IMAGES
of Rail

THE MONON RAILROAD IN SOUTHERN INDIANA

BLOOMINGTON CELEBRATES THE MONON CENTENNIAL. This image was taken in July 1947, as the Monon Railroad was celebrating its 100th anniversary. This celebration lasted a good part of a week in many of the towns and cities from Michigan City south to New Albany. The center of attention was the Civil War steam locomotive the *General*, which was at the Monon depot. (Courtesy of the Monroe County Historical Society Museum.)

On the cover: Please see page 69. (Courtesy of Larry Pritchett.)

IMAGES
of Rail

THE MONON RAILROAD IN SOUTHERN INDIANA

David E. Longest

ARCADIA
PUBLISHING

Published by Arcadia Publishing
Charleston, South Carolina

Library of Congress Catalog Card Number: 2007943378

For all general information contact Arcadia Publishing at:
Telephone 843-853-2070
Fax 843-853-0044
E-mail sales@arcadiapublishing.com
For customer service and orders:
Toll-Free 1-888-313-2665

Visit us on the Internet at www.arcadiapublishing.com

*I dedicate this book to all the former Monon Railroad
employees and their families. I also dedicate this book to the former
employees of the countless businesses and industries that were served by
the Monon Railroad. Your efforts and contributions to Indiana
and our nation have not been forgotten.*

CONTENTS

ACKNOWLEDGMENTS

This book is intended to remember the Monon Railroad, its many workers, and the thousands of people touched by its service from New Albany to Bloomington and from Orleans west to French Lick. I am going to express my thanks as I acknowledge the individual communities showcased in the book.

I wish to thank my hometown, New Albany, for its heritage with the Monon Railroad. I thank the librarians of the Indiana Room at the New Albany-Floyd County Public Library for their help as they provide outstanding assistance in guiding researchers through the many resources available. I also thank Bill Hacker, Jim Berry, John Hartline, and Bob Wolfe for their images and assistance. I want to acknowledge certain individuals and the currently active industries that they represent: Bob Streepey of B. L. Curry and Sons and Bill Nunn of L. Thorn Company, for their tremendous assistance. I also thank Dave Binford, who provided me with information and images of the Hoosier Panel Company.

In the Borden and Pekin communities, I want to thank the following for use of their images: the Borden Library, Albert Hunt, Larry Johnson, and the Pekin Town Hall. I am also grateful to current employer Kimball International and its employee Bill Reuss for his help.

I thank the Stevens Museum in Salem for help in providing images of businesses that were an important part of that town's past. I also acknowledge Cecil Smith and David Gottbrath for providing me valuable information.

In researching the communities of Orleans and Paoli in Orange County, I received great assistance from Robert F. Henderson Jr., Wilma Davis, Duane Radcliff, Bud Farlow, Larry Pritchett, Brenda Cornwell, and the Paoli City Hall.

In researching the Bedford community, I found excellent help at the Lawrence County Museum. I am grateful especially to Joyce Shepherd for her help and cooperation. I also want to thank Michele Kirkman of Elite Tours, Inc., for providing helpful learning opportunities.

I thank and acknowledge the efforts of the Monroe County Historical Society Museum. Bloomington businessman John Bender was also quite helpful with photographs and information about the Bender Lumber Company.

I also thank and acknowledge the work of the following photographers or collectors of old photographs: George Lortz, Tom Rankin, Tim Swan, George Carpenter, Dave Ritenour, Ron Marquardt, Dick Fontaine, Steve Stafford, and Jim Craig. I also recognize the support and contributions of the Monon Railroad Historical-Technical Society. Images belonging to the Monon Railroad Historical-Technical Society will be abbreviated as MRHTS. Unless otherwise noted, images are from my personal collection.

INTRODUCTION

The story of the Monon Railroad begins with the reader having a basic knowledge of its first president, James Brooks. What is now referred to as the Monon Railroad began as a simple business venture. In a day when canals were still vogue, James Brooks was impressed with the possibilities of bringing the iron horse to New Albany. Brooks was a very ambitious citizen who had moved into New Albany, a river town, from another river town, Cincinnati. Somewhere along the way he developed a vision to transform New Albany and alter forever the face of the countryside of southern and northwestern Indiana.

James Brooks was born in Orrington, Maine, in 1810, and his family moved to Cincinnati when he was a youngster. In the 1820s, Brooks moved downstream to New Albany, just west of the Ohio River Falls. At the time, Indiana was in a rather heated competition over which state, Kentucky or Indiana, might receive approval and funds to build a canal on the Ohio River, near the falls. The competition was won by Kentucky, and in 1830, the Louisville and Portland Canal was built on the Kentucky side of the Ohio River. This new canal became a boom for Louisville as it encouraged growth and in time improved trade revenue. As a result, Louisville began growing at a rate above that of New Albany. Brooks felt that a railroad could help offset this revenue loss that New Albany incurred.

In January 1847, the Indiana legislature passed an act stating that the road from New Albany to Salem may be completed as a railroad by a private individual. In the spring of 1847, the New Albany and Salem Railroad (NA&SRR) was chartered in Providence, now called Borden, with James Brooks and six other men. When the details were ironed out, Brooks became the first president.

By January 1851, the NA&SRR had reached Salem, a distance of about 30 miles. Three months later the NA&SRR reached Bedford. And by October 1853, the young railroad had tracks completed to Bloomington. By 1854, it stretched from the Ohio River to the Great Lakes at Michigan City. In 1859, a drought had affected the railroad's revenues and the railroad was forced to reorganize. After the reorganization, the name was changed to the Louisville, New Albany and Chicago Railroad Company (LNA&C).

The railroad grew more with its consolidation with the Indianapolis and Chicago Air Line in 1881. Now the railroad traveled in two directions: north from New Albany to Michigan City and from Indianapolis to Chicago. This allowed the Monon to enter the huge market of Chicago. By 1897, the LNA&C was reorganized as the Chicago, Indianapolis and Louisville Railway (CI&L). This was the last name change until the railroad was officially called the Monon in 1956.

This book will review the Monon and some of the businesses and industries that it served beginning in New Albany and ending in the Bloomington area. It will also review the Monon's presence in the communities west of Orleans: Paoli, West Baden, and French Lick.

During the early 20th century, New Albany became a major producer of plywood and veneer. By 1920, New Albany produced more plywood than any other community in the world with companies such as Indiana Veneer and Panel Company, New Albany Veneering Company, Breece Plywood Company (interchanged with the Monon), Chester B. Stem, and Hoosier Panel Company.

In Salem, Orleans, and Paoli, industries were born that were making the most of the excellent local hardwood forests found in southern Indiana. These towns were producing chairs, tabletops, and other pieces of furniture that put them on the map. These communities learned early on that they had to use the resources found in their environment to allow their towns to flourish and grow.

The same was very true of the communities of Bedford, Bloomington, and other smaller towns nearby. Limestone was the resource that was there for the taking. One must understand, though, that the taking was not easy. The removal of the precious stone from the ground is a story in itself that well exhibits the evolution of specialized tools and machinery. The Monon Railroad had a vital role in transporting the huge blocks from the quarry to the mill and from the mill to the consumer.

The varied companies in southern Indiana were as dependent on the Monon Railroad as the railroad was dependent upon the industries. Railroads were so important to a community that towns would feverishly accumulate funds as to entice a railroad to build in their town. Purposeful and driven men looked for ways to make money in manufacturing, but if that town had a railroad, there was less concern then with the product getting to market.

A look at West Baden and French Lick puts an entirely different face on the Monon Railroad's traditional role of servicing southern Indiana industries. In these two towns, service was what it was about. The huge hotels and resorts that developed around the natural springs of these areas were all about service. That was the product—people kicking back and being serviced. One found few factories in these communities, but one did find people who wanted to get away and relax and maybe get healthier while away. The Monon promoted the tourist industry in French Lick and West Baden, although it did not always prove to be financially lucrative.

This book is a look at many of the industries and businesses that the Monon served and served well. Some were huge in size; many were not, but the Monon met their needs as a transporter of raw materials, manufactured products, and people. This book examines how the Monon Railroad economically and socially met the needs of businesses and people of southern Indiana.

One

THE MONON IN
NEW ALBANY

NEW ALBANY AND SALEM RAILROAD DEPOT. This image shows the original New Albany and Salem Railroad depot, which was built around 1851. At the time that this photograph was taken in 1897, the New Albany and Salem Railroad was called the Chicago, Indianapolis and Louisville Railroad (CI&L). The CI&L used this structure until 1891, six years after the completion of the Kentucky and Indiana (K&I) bridge. (Courtesy of Jim Berry.)

LOUIS HARTMAN AND SONS. The Louis Hartman and Sons Company used the Monon Railroad depot after M. Zier and Company vacated the structure. The Monon shipped sugar, stock feeds, poultry feeds, shortening, and flour to Hartman and Sons. From 1958 to 1960, Hartman and Sons received an average of 132 train cars annually by the Monon Railroad. This image was taken in the early 1950s. (Courtesy of the New Albany-Floyd County Public Library.)

CALL AND SEE

Louis Hartman & Sons

DURING CENTENNIAL

Occupying Original
M O N O N
Passenger and Freight Building
which we have occupied
nearly one-half century

PILSBURY FLOUR
Sugar - Shortening - Mazola Oil
Full Line of Stock and Poultry Feeds

HARTMAN AND SON ADVERTISEMENT. This advertisement is from a booklet that was used during the Monon Railroad centennial celebration in New Albany in July 1947. Many communities served by the Monon had similar booklets composed that outlined the various events related to the celebration. The advertisement states that Hartman and Sons had occupied that old depot for nearly 50 years. (Courtesy of Monon Centennial Booklet.)

10

HOME OF JAMES BROOKS. In the spring of 1847, James Brooks and six constituents, W. C. DePauw, John Gordon, John Davis, V. C. Campbell, Samuel Reid, and Henry Shields, met in Providence and formed the New Albany and Salem Railroad. Brooks became the first president and remained president until his resignation in 1859, after the railroad met with financial difficulties. This photograph shows his home in New Albany, located on East Ninth Street.

NEW ALBANY AND SALEM DEPOT. The image shows the rear view of the New Albany and Salem Railroad terminal station that is shown on page 9. This photograph was taken in 1897 and shows a caboose in the station. Several tracks of the Monon train yard can be seen moving toward the terminal depot. (Courtesy of Jim Berry.)

MONON PASSENGER DEPOT. This image shows the second passenger depot that the Monon Railroad constructed in New Albany. It was located on the northeast corner of East Main Street and Vincennes Street. It was built in 1884 and was used until around 1937. Its construction coincided with the opening of the K&I bridge the same year. This location proved better for passengers than the Oak Street depot. (Courtesy of the New Albany-Floyd County Public Library.)

MONON MAIL CARS. This view of the depot was taken in May 1955, from the west side of the wooden freight house. At this time, Monon freight and passenger trains were originating and terminating in Louisville, but a brief, weeklong strike by the workers of the Louisville and Nashville Railroad resulted in the train operations moving to New Albany. This strike lasted from April 30 to May 4, 1955. (Courtesy of Jim Berry.)

APPROACHING THE DAISY DEPOT. This image, taken from the cab of a Monon freight train, shows the Daisy depot on the right. This was first used as a streetcar waiting area and after the demise of streetcars was used by Home Transit, Inc., bus service. Patrons using the Daisy Bus Line, which connected to Louisville, also shared the building. If one follows the curve, one will approach the K&I terminal bridge. (Courtesy of Dave Ritenour.)

PENNSYLVANIA RAILROAD BRIDGE. In 1882, the Monon contracted with the Pennsylvania Railroad to use five miles of its track. This allowed the Monon to connect closer to the Louisville bridge at Jeffersonville. The Monon later contracted with the Louisville Bridge and Depot Company so that it could enter Louisville on the Pennsylvania Railroad bridge. This image shows the Pennsylvania Railroad bridge that was built in 1870 and used by the Monon.

K&I Bridge. The K&I bridge, which opened in 1886, would now connect New Albany to Louisville by rail and pedestrian traffic. In 1889, the Monon Railroad signed an agreement to use the K&I bridge, ending the Monon's need to enter Louisville through Jeffersonville. This image shows the New Albany shoreline, the first K&I bridge, and the construction of the second K&I bridge in the foreground. (Courtesy of John Hartline and Bob Lawson.)

Bridge to Louisville. This 1971 photograph shows the New Albany entrance to the ramp of the K&I terminal bridge. The image was taken from the cab of Monon train No. 71 as it approaches the crossing of Main Street. The Baltimore and Ohio Railroad and the Southern Railway were then using the track on the left. To the right of the Monon track is the IV Tower, where trains received their orders. (Courtesy of Dave Ritenour.)

STREET RUNNING. In this photograph, Monon train No. 71 travels south on Fifteenth Street in New Albany in what was called "street running." For the train's engineer, there was always a concern for drivers not waiting for the train to pass and the possibility that they might get too close to the passing train. Street running also occurred in Bedford, Bloomington, and Lafayette. (Courtesy of Dave Ritenour.)

MONON SWITCH ENGINE NO. 5. This Monon switch engine is shown here in the Monon yard off Culbertson Avenue. This diesel engine had 600 horsepower and was purchased by the Monon in August 1949. The switch engine's job was to handle all the cars out of Louisville's Youngstown yard, complete all track and industrial work, and line up cars that were ready to be picked up. (Courtesy of Jim Berry.)

MONON F-3 ENGINE. This photograph shows the second CI&L freight house with a Monon Railroad F-3 diesel locomotive to the right. This diesel was purchased by the Monon in May 1947 to be used with passenger units. It had 1,500 horsepower and was part of the Monon's effort to move from steam locomotives to diesels. (Courtesy of the New Albany-Floyd County Public Library.)

MONON FREIGHT HOUSE. The Monon Railroad's second freight house was constructed around 1896 and used until around 1963. It was built on Culbertson Avenue, previously called Sycamore Street. It was a wooden building that sat parallel to the CI&L tracks at the intersection of Culbertson Avenue and Bank Street. This image shows the interior of that building and five railroad employees. (Courtesy of Jim Berry.)

MONON FREIGHT AGENT. This photograph shows Monon freight agent Walter E. Jenks in front of the wooden freight house at 201 Culbertson Avenue. The delivery of packages and parcels by train in 1920 might be compared to today's deliveries by Federal Express, minus the convenience of it coming directly to the front door. (Courtesy of Jim Berry.)

THE GENERAL. The famous Civil War steam engine the *General* was in New Albany for the city's sesquicentennial celebration in 1963. Here it is shown to the left of the third Monon freight house. This new freight house, built in 1963, allowed for several Monon office employees to return to New Albany from offices they were using in Louisville. In this image, freight agent Walter E. Jenks admires the old engine. (Courtesy of Jim Berry.)

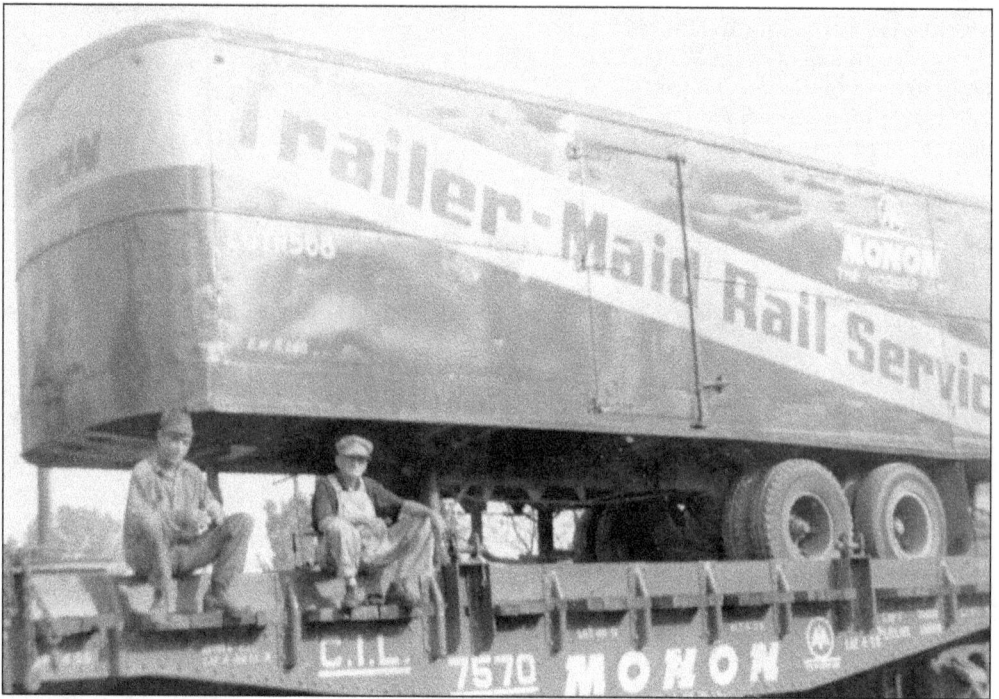

PIGGYBACK RAIL SERVICE. Trailer-Maid Rail Service was the name given the Monon Railroad's piggyback service whereby semitrailers were carried on flatcars. Railroads had to construct special ramps so that the trailers could be loaded onto the flatcars. This 1955 image was taken by Howard Tegart and shows such a ramp on East Fourth Street in the train yard. The men are, from left to right, Mose Singleton (section man) and Chester Scott (car inspector). (Courtesy of Jim Berry.)

THE HOOSIER LINE. This F-3 engine, No. 82, was purchased in May 1947. These engines were produced by Electro-Motive and were equipped with 1,500-horsepower diesel engines. This unit was painted in the red, white, and gray Monon color scheme. This image was taken in New Albany's Monon train yard. (Courtesy of Jim Berry.)

18

BEST FRIEND OF CHARLESTON. In July 1947, the Monon centennial brought four days of events to several Hoosier cities, including New Albany. In this photograph, Monon freight agent Walter E. Jenks (right) and an unidentified man stand in front of the replica of famed engine the *Best Friend of Charleston*. The original engine was built for the South Carolina Railroad and Canal Company in 1830. (Courtesy of Jim Berry.)

THE WILLIAM MASON. New Albany was very involved in the Monon centennial of 1947. This photograph shows Monon president John Barriger in the cab of the *William Mason*. The steam locomotive was borrowed from the Baltimore and Ohio Railroad and traveled from Hammond to New Albany for this time of reflection and celebration. The *William Mason* was built in 1856 and was rebuilt in 1926. (Courtesy of the MRHTS.)

SCHULTZ DUSTLESS COAL. The Schultz Coal Company was located on Pearl Street near the Monon Railroad train yard. This photograph shows the coal yard underwater during the 1937 flood. The sign above the office tells customers that they could purchase dustless coal. The Monon Railroad delivered an average of 410 cars of coal to the Schultz Coal Company in the late 1950s. Much of this coal came from eastern Kentucky. The Schultz Coal Company continued in New Albany through the 1950s. In 1958, the coal business changed greatly with the arrival of natural gas through the Texas Transmission Company. Gas furnaces basically put the coal companies out of business by causing a great decline in the usage of coal in households. It brought great pleasure to the author to not have to fill the coal bucket each day after school. However, he did miss watching the delivery of coal as it was moved by conveyor through the garage coal chute. (Courtesy of the New Albany-Floyd County Public Library.)

HONEY-KRUST BREAD. This photograph shows an advertisement for Honey-Krust Bread. Long before aromatherapy, many children would gain a warm and secure feeling from smelling the baking bread while walking near the bakery on Pearl Street while downtown. The Monon Railroad shipped about 45 cars annually to Rainbo in the late 1950s. (Courtesy of Monon Centennial Booklet.)

For The Right Bread
Call For

HONEY-KRUST BREAD
PURE MILK · REAL HONEY

Congratulations to
The MONON on Its
100th Birthday

RAINBO BREAD. This building on Pearl Street housed Honey-Krust Bread Company for many years and in later years was the home of Rainbo Bread. In the New Albany plant, the bakery only produced buns and special breads in the 1960s. Regular loaves of bread were then being produced in Louisville. Rainbo Baking Company left New Albany in late 1967 and moved to the Louisville Rainbo plant. (Courtesy of the New Albany-Floyd County Public Library.)

MONON VENEER AND LUMBER COMPANY ADVERTISEMENT. This advertisement, acknowledging one of New Albany's older industries, was placed in the New Albany Monon centennial events booklet during the 1947 centennial celebration. The Monon Veneer and Lumber Company was at 1014 East Sixth Street in New Albany from 1920 until it sold to B. L. Curry in 1953. (Courtesy of Monon Centennial Booklet.)

B. L. CURRY AND SONS, INC. In 1953, B. L. Curry acquired the Monon Veneer and Lumber Company property from owner Virgil Theiss. Curry began veneer production the next year. This image of the Curry property on East Sixth Street shows the factory and what some people believe is the Monon Railroad's second roundhouse built in New Albany. The roundhouse, now demolished, is to the far right of the cluster of veneer producing buildings. (Courtesy of B. L. Curry and Sons.)

MONON'S SECOND ROUNDHOUSE. This more recent view of the B. L. Curry and Sons property shows what may have been a second Monon roundhouse to the left of the factory buildings. A 1956 Sanborn map labeled the building as being a mill room. Curry and Sons shipped by the Monon Railroad an average of 46 cars from its plant from 1958 to 1960, and it received from the Monon an average of 142 train cars annually during the same period. (Courtesy of B. L. Curry and Sons.)

ANCHOR STOVE AND RANGE COMPANY. Anchor Stove and Range Company, located on Culbertson Avenue, was founded in 1865 as Terstegge-Gohmann and Company. When Anchor began, its address was 300 Sycamore Street. In the late 1890s, Sycamore Street was renamed Culbertson Avenue. This image taken around the 1930s shows a Monon boxcar on the factory siding and the Monon freight house in the lower left corner. (Courtesy of the New Albany-Floyd County Public Library.)

23

ANCHOR-PADGETT BUILDING. In the 1950s, Anchor Stove and Range Company was a division of Stratton and Terstegge Company. In October 1963, Stratton and Terstegge was producing items such as fireplace fixtures and garden furniture. This image shows the same building as it looks today. James Padgett now owns the factory building and other nearby properties, including the land that once held the first Monon Railroad depot and the Monon train yard.

MONON FREIGHT HOUSE SITE. Several years ago, James Padgett placed this caboose in front of the main entrance to his business, Padgett, Inc., to mark the location of the Monon freight house. In July 2007, a state marker was placed in front of this caboose to commemorate the site as it relates to the Monon Railroad's contribution to the Underground Railroad in the southern part of Indiana.

KAHLER COMPANY. In 1907, the Kahler Company was organized and soon began operations at the northwest corner of Pearl and Oak Streets. That structure, shown here in 2001, is now being refurbished. The Kahler Company's initial officers included Ferdinand Kahler, president, August Kahler, Joseph Kahler. Initially the plant produced office and residential tabletops, and by 1909, it was producing automobile beds. It was at this site until about 1910.

TORNADO DESTROYS THE KAHLER PLANT. Around 1911, the Kahler Company moved its operations to Vincennes Street, west of Charlestown Road. It appears that the Kahler Company was using property on both sides of the Monon track, on Vincennes Street. In 1917, a tornado destroyed the Kahler plant. In January 1917, Kahler was manufacturing automobile bodies for the Ford Motor Company. (Courtesy of the New Albany-Floyd County Public Library.)

NATIONAL HOMES CORPORATION. After the 1917 tornado, the Kahler Company decided to stay in New Albany and rebuild. In 1918, Kahler rebuilt at the corner of Grant Line Road and Vincennes Street, west of the Monon Railroad tracks. The Kahler Company remained in this building from 1917 to 1959, when National Homes Corporation began producing kitchen cabinets. In 1959 and 1960, National Homes shipped on the Monon an average of 130 railcars annually.

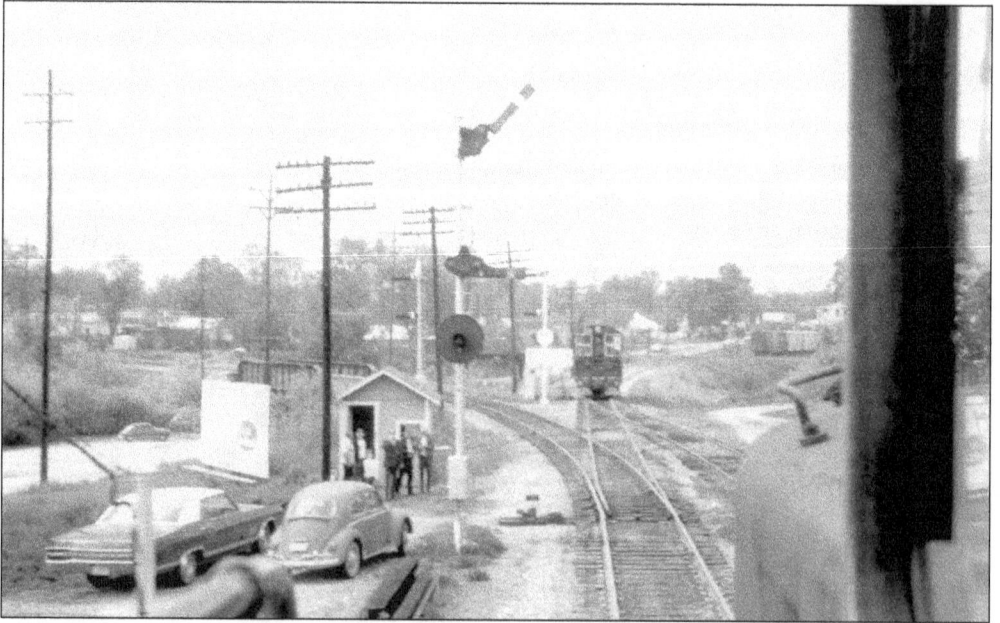

NEW ALBANY WYE. This 1971 image shows the New Albany wye as taken from the cab of train No. 71. The track that curves to the left will proceed toward the K&I bridge. The track straight ahead continues toward the Monon freight house on Culbertson Avenue. In the center of the image can be seen the two viaducts crossing East Eighth Street. (Courtesy of Dave Ritenour.)

L. Thorn and Company. L. Thorn and Company first opened in 1917, and the entrance to the plant was off Clark Street. The Monon had a siding into the Thorn brickyard, and the Monon tracks ran west of the property. This image shows this initial building site with the office. At that time, the industry produced concrete blocks and ornamental concrete products. (Courtesy of Bill Hacker.)

Moving Concrete Blocks. This image shows a Yale brand lift being operated by Clarence Robinson, employee of L. Thorn and Company. Such machinery took the place of a few workers, but what an improved way of transporting loads of block and brick in the building materials yard. This photograph shows the back of the office building shown in the previous image. (Courtesy of Bill Hacker.)

27

L. THORN AND COMPANY ON VINCENNES STREET. In 1939, L. Thorn and Company moved around the corner to 1319 Vincennes Street. This move allowed for an easier entrance to the property, room for product expansion, and the addition of more modern equipment. As the sign designates, Thorn sold concrete blocks, columns, drains, flower vases, sundials, and birdbaths. L. Thorn has been a fixture in New Albany for nearly a century. (Courtesy of Bill Hacker.)

THORN COMPANY AERIAL VIEW. This aerial photograph gives a good view of the L. Thorn Company's second property. The property can be seen in the lower left of the photograph with family dwellings across each side of the main entrance. Vincennes Street can be seen north of the plant and crossing the Monon Railroad tracks. The large building to the left of the tracks is the Kahler Company factory. (Courtesy of L. Thorn Company.)

L. THORN STORAGE FACILITY. As the company grew, need arose for there to be more room for block production and for storage. This additional Thorn property was located north of the Vincennes Street property on Vance Avenue, near the Monon tracks. This photograph shows a line of boxcars on the L. Thorn rail siding. (Courtesy of L. Thorn Company.)

L. THORN COMPANY. Today L. Thorn Company has this plant and yard operation on State Road 111, on the east side of where the CSX rail line crosses the highway. It still has some need for a rail siding and occasionally receives brick by rail. However, more brick is moved by truck today than by rail since trucks are able to meet the needs of brickyards and building sites more expediently.

HOOSIER PANEL COMPANY. The Hoosier Panel Company was incorporated in 1915 and began operations in early 1916 in this new building. A February 1916 *New Albany Ledger* article stated that work on the new plant was progressing despite the weather, which had included severe flooding. The plant was expected to employ about 125 workers. Sam Stout, principal investor, offered A. O. Binford the opportunity to manage one of the three plywood factories that he owned in the Louisville area. These included the Indiana Panel Company and the Hoosier Panel Company, both located in New Albany, and the Crescent Panel Company located in Louisville, Kentucky. Binford chose the Hoosier Panel Company. In World War I, the company made plywood for use in American aircraft. This image shows an aerial view of the factory looking northwest and shows a great look at the length of the spur line running between plant buildings. (Courtesy of Dave Binford.)

BELT SANDER OPERATOR. The Hoosier Panel Company was famous within the ranks of those producing quality plywood panels. A. O. Binford had even served the industry as president of the National Plywood Association. Such panels were made of hardwood plywood and used in television cabinets, wood kitchen cabinets, stereo cabinets, pianos, organs, and other wood products. This image shows belt sander operator Max Longest. (Courtesy of Lois Longest.)

HOOSIER PANEL PLANT. This photograph was taken in May 1987. It shows the Monon Railroad tracks and the factory name. On the right of the image can be seen the break between buildings, where the spur line ran. The plant helped perfect the use of hot-plate presses, resin adhesives, and other benchmark advances in plywood production during its 70 years in operation. (Courtesy of Lois Longest.)

CHESTER B. STEM COMPANY. This old photograph shows the main office of the Chester B. Stem property on Grant Line Road. As a youth, one of the author's fondest memories of the Stem factory was a tall totem pole displayed on the front lawn. The pole related to the rich forests of the Pacific Northwest. (Courtesy of Bill Hacker.)

STEM DRYING YARD. From 1958 to 1960, the Monon Railroad shipped an average of 119 train cars per year of finished product from Chester B. Stem, Inc. During the same period, the Monon annually delivered an average of 306 trainloads of logs such as mahogany, East India rosewood, teak, and other fine woods. The yard area in this photograph shows the continuous air drying that some customers prefer.

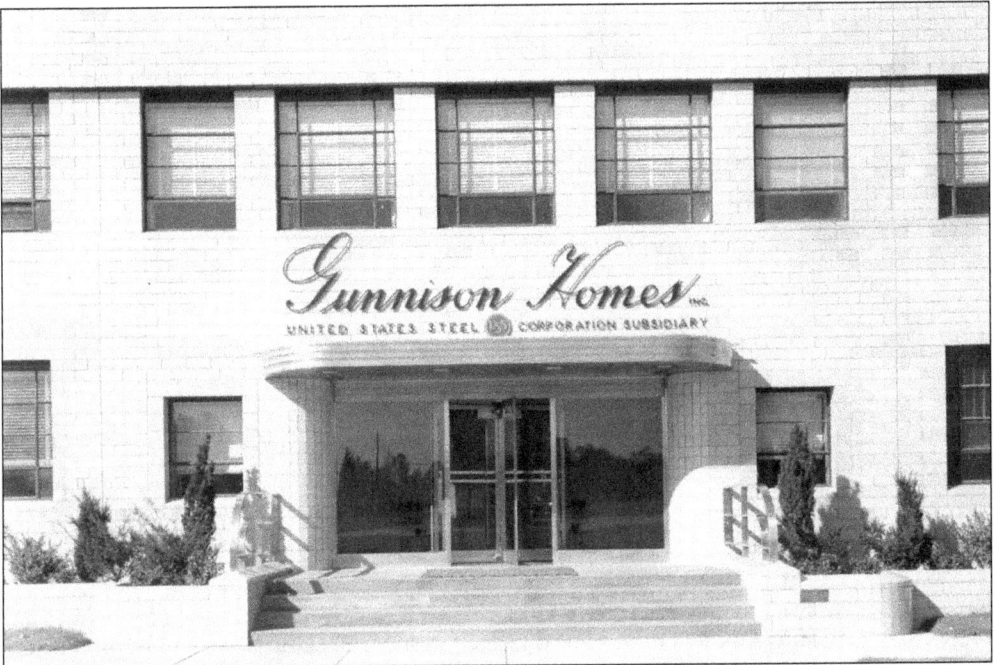

GUNNISON CUSTOMER ENTRANCE. Gunnison Housing Corporation was formed in the 1930s by Foster Gunnison. By 1937, Gunnison's prefabricated homes business was quite popular in some regions of the Midwest. This plant was newly constructed around 1946 for Gunnison Housing Corporation. Up to that time, the company had been using a portion of the Breece Veneer Company on East Thirteenth Street. (Courtesy of the New Albany-Floyd County Public Library.)

GUNNISON DUST COLLECTOR. This image shows the dust collector system used by Gunnison Housing Corporation for removal of dust from the sawing of gypsum board. Sawdust was burned in those days. The dump truck was used to remove certain types of refuse from the factory. The pickup truck was used for local deliveries. (Courtesy of the New Albany-Floyd County Public Library.)

GUNNISON SHIPPING DOCK. This dock was located west of the plant. Several Gunnison trucks are lined up in the process of being loaded with the prefabricated home packages. Gunnison Housing Corporation began using this new plant in 1946, after World War II ended. (Courtesy of the New Albany-Floyd County Public Library.)

GUNNISON RAIL PLATFORM. This image shows workers loading a boxcar with banded trim for use in home construction. In the foreground are Coleman floor furnaces. Some of these heating units were installed overhead, using an updraft for pulling air into the furnace, while others were placed on the floor. (Courtesy of the New Albany-Floyd County Public Library.)

GUNNISON MILL ROOM. This photograph shows some of the wood-milling machines used to cut and size lumber for use in prefabricated wall units. To the left is an electric load transporter. These portable movers could lift loads quickly and in less space than a forklift might be able to manipulate. (Courtesy of the New Albany-Floyd County Public Library.)

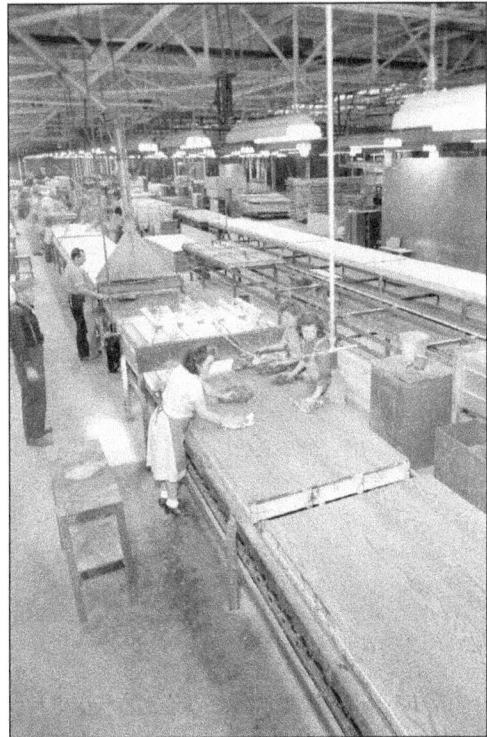

GUNNISON FLOORING ASSEMBLY LINE. This image shows the type of assembly line that one would see throughout much of the Gunnison plant. The ladies are applying a coat of wood stain to the floor unit. Farther up the line there was an infrared light that would dry the stain. These wood panels were produced less than a mile away at the Hoosier Panel Company. (Courtesy of the New Albany-Floyd County Public Library.)

PERIOD CABINET COMPANY. On Eighth Street in New Albany stands the former factory site of the Robinson-Nugent Company; however, this building was used in the 1930s by the Period Cabinet Company, which produced wood cabinets. Period was a Monon Railroad customer, and its location was within a half mile of the Monon wye on East Eighth Street.

M. FINE AND SONS. M. Fine and Sons is located at 1500 East Main Street and began operation in 1922. This image shows the M. Fine and Sons rail siding. Fine was not on the Monon rail line but did interchange with the Pennsylvania Railroad so that it could ship and deliver as needed. The Fine company manufactured clothing, especially pants and shirts.

H. A. SEINSHEIMER AND COMPANY. H. A. Seinsheimer and Company was another of New Albany's producers of fine clothing, including men's topcoats and suits. The Seinsheimer building is located at 1502 Beeler Street, extending to the corner at East Fifteenth Street. H. A. Seinsheimer began operations in 1925. The factory employed 700 workers in the 1950s. The factory was on the Monon Railroad line.

407   13th and River, New Albany.   Breece Veneer Co. in center.

J. T. BREECE VENEER COMPANY. In 1937, Breece Veneer Company began using the vacated New Albany Veneer Company building at Thirteenth Street and McBeth Street. This postcard shows that factory site under a great amount of water during the 1937 flood. The Monon Railroad interchanged with the Southern Railway in making switches for Breece Veneer Company. (Courtesy of the Julian R. Fisher Company.)

PILLSBURY REFRIGERATION PLANT. In 1869, Charles Pillsbury founded the Pillsbury Flour Mills Company. In 1931, Louisville baker Lively Willoughby began selling his idea of preparing uncooked biscuits that could be stored in iceboxes. He had created a method of wrapping the biscuit dough in tinfoil and storing the dough under pressure in paper tubes. This led to the product known today as popping-fresh dough. This image shows the Pillsbury plant.

MCDONALD'S GRAIN ELEVATOR. When Monon Railroad engineers had to perform interchanges with the Southern Railway, they would see this New Albany landmark north of the flood wall. McDonald's Grain Elevator has stood along New Albany's shoreline for nearly a century. It is named for John McDonald, president of the company.

Two

THE MONON IN BORDEN

BORDEN MONON DEPOT. Beginning under the leadership of James Brooks, the New Albany and Salem Railroad had its start in 1847 at Providence, now called Borden. It was here that he met with six associates and organized what became the Monon Railroad. This image shows the Borden depot. (Courtesy of the Harry Jackson collection.)

DIESEL HEADING SOUTH. This Indiana Rail Road (INRD) train is passing through Borden near the site of where the Monon Railroad depot stood. The depot was torn down in the 1970s. The INRD trains are seen quite often on trackage between Louisville and Bedford. Engines No. 6013 and No. 6009 are pulling this train. This image was taken in November 2007.

BORDEN INSTITUTE. William W. Borden was born in 1823 in Providence. In 1883, he founded the Borden Institute because he wanted to give area youth a liberal arts education. Some students of the institute used the Monon Railroad to commute. In 1905, the institute became Borden High School, which it remained until 1955. In 1973, the building was placed on the National Register of Historic Places, and it was demolished in 1983. (Courtesy of Larry Johnson.)

STRAWBERRY TIME IN BORDEN. The berry and produce business of the Borden community was quite dependent upon the Monon Railroad to transport the berries to market. Borden and neighboring Pekin were once the largest berry-shipping point in Indiana. This 1925 image shows boxes of strawberries being loaded on a train car. These berries were brought to the depot by many locals in many modes of transport, including horse- or mule-drawn wagons. These berries were shipped via Railway Express in refrigerator cars to Chicago where they were distributed to other major markets. A Monon northbound passenger train would stop at Borden at about 10:00 p.m. and pick up as many as six to eight of these refrigerator cars and proceed north. Soon after the strawberries were harvested in late May, blackberries and raspberries followed, making it a full berry season. (Courtesy of Larry Johnson.)

BORDEN BERRIES. This image shows a crate label like the ones that were attached to the crates as the berries were packed for shipment. H. C. Littell was the initial manager of the Borden-Pekin Fruit Growers' Association, a group that was instrumental in promoting the area's produce. At one time, the berries was the mascot of Borden High School. (Courtesy of Don Maier.)

BORDEN LOG MILL WORKERS. This photograph shows posed employees at a Borden lumber mill many years ago. In the lower portion of the image can be seen the rail used to either move logs into the lumberyard or for removing the cut lumber. A horse-drawn wagon loaded with lumber can be seen in the far right of the photograph. (Courtesy of Larry Johnson.)

BORDEN CABINET COMPANY. This aerial photograph shows the first Borden Cabinet plant, which was then Borden's only industry. In 1952, the Jasper Corporation purchased the Borden Cabinet Company, allowing Borden Cabinet to retain its name. A fire destroyed the 50,000-square-foot structure in 1962. The Monon Railroad line is in the lower left of the photograph. A rail siding can be seen arcing into the center of the factory complex. (Courtesy of Larry Johnson.)

BORDEN CABINET WORKERS. This undated image shows a group of Borden Cabinet workers gathered for a group photograph. One can only speculate the purpose of the gathering—maybe a company anniversary, maybe a company success story. The plant employed approximately 195 in 1962 when fire destroyed it. In the back row, fourth from the left, is Harry Jackson. (Courtesy of Larry Johnson.)

CABINET CONSTRUCTION. The Borden Cabinet Company produced radio and television cabinets for many years. This cabinet is in a case clamp, used to secure the cabinet while being produced. The glue used to secure the panel to the cabinet was activated by a high frequency, which produces heat. This image shows Albert Hunt watching Charlie Lockenour as he works with the cabinet. (Courtesy of Albert Hunt.)

PREPARING THE SURFACE. This photograph shows Albert Hunt, Borden Cabinet Company retiree, watching Danny Thompson as he uses a polisher on a television cabinet. The cabinet was made of poplar wood with a Masonite printed surface. In the late 1950s, Borden Cabinet shipped products on the Monon Railroad, averaging 225 boxcars annually. The Monon delivered an average of 39 railcars of materials to Borden Cabinet those same years. (Courtesy of Albert Hunt.)

NEW BORDEN CABINET PLANT. An enlarged Borden Cabinet plant was dedicated on October 12, 1962. The new plant had 85,000 square feet and was to employ 240 people. Fire walls had been constructed into the design to help eliminate the chance for the type of fire that took the old structure. This aerial photograph shows the plant and the Monon Railroad tracks and siding north of the factory. (Courtesy of Kimball International.)

KIMBALL INTERNATIONAL AERIAL VIEW. In 1980, the Kimball National Office Furniture Division was begun to manufacture furniture. The former Monon rail line is hidden by the plant, and the plant uses trucks instead of the railroad. Today the Borden factory wears the name Kimball International, a very familiar name in southern Indiana and parts of Kentucky. This image shows the sprawl of the plant as it has grown since construction in 1962. (Courtesy of Kimball International.)

STEAM LOCOMOTIVE PULLING THE KNOBS. This image was taken around 1900 and shows Monon No. 203 climbing the "knobs" between Borden and Pekin. At this time, the Monon Railroad was the CI&L. This engine had a 4-8-0 wheel configuration. Notice the black smoke puffing from the engine's boiler as the challenge of the hill's grade is met. (Courtesy of the Pekin Town Hall.)

DIESEL PULLING THE KNOB. This photograph taken in 1964 shows Monon diesel No. 400, an Alco C-628 road switcher, leading a train north of Borden. This train is ascending the knob, which stretches for five to six miles and was one of the Monon's steepest grades. The grade required the Monon to assign a helper engine to be at Borden on a 24-hour-a-day basis to help make it up the grade. (Courtesy of the MRHTS, Charles Huffer Collection.)

FIRST PEKIN MONON DEPOT. In 1851, the first Monon train went through Pekin, and around 1900, W. A. Graves built the first depot in Pekin. The emergence of the railroad allowed Washington County patrons to board or get off at any one of eight stations without leaving the county. Some of the other Washington County stops were Farabee, Harristown, and Hitchcock. This image shows a steam engine at the Pekin depot. (Courtesy of the Stevens Memorial Museum.)

MONON DEPOT AT PEKIN. This Pekin depot was built around 1915 but had been abandoned when this photograph was taken in the mid-1970s, after which it was torn down. Many Washington County residents were associated with the railroad in depending on its services or as an employee on a train, as a section hand, or at a local station. (Courtesy of Cecil Smith.)

PEKIN RAIL LINE. This photograph taken in the 1920s shows CI&L boxcar No. 17089 sitting with another boxcar on the Pekin siding. To the far left is the Monon Railroad depot that was built in 1915. The Monon shipped large quantities of lumber, livestock, and milk from Pekin. (Courtesy of the Pekin Town Hall.)

JOHN T. J. GRAVES. In December 1900, this two-story stone building was constructed north of the Monon tracks. John T. J. Graves and his brother operated an implement and hardware business in the building until May 1911, when it was sold to G. M. Johnson and his son Alfred. This image shows the rail siding with a boxcar. On the far right is another business where milk cans were distributed. (Courtesy of the MRHTS.)

G. M. JOHNSON AND SONS. In 1914, Alfred Johnson took over the hardware business and operated it until his death in 1956. It was sold to Ralph Callum in 1958, and he converted the business into a variety store. This image shows a flatcar on the siding. At one time there were stock pens behind the Johnson building. (Courtesy of the MRHTS.)

SULLIVAN FEED MILL. The Sullivan family still operates this farm supply business, which is located on the north side of the former Monon Railroad tracks. Clair Sullivan started in the feed business around 1941. The building shown in the photograph was built in 1946. In the late 1950s, Sullivan Feed Mill received an average of 24 railcars from the Monon Railroad. Today the mill continues to sell seed, farm implements, hardware, and garden needs.

O. L. CAUBLE WAREHOUSE. This old building is the O. L. Cauble warehouse. In 1940, the Washington County Farm Bureau Cooperative Association bought the warehouse to use as its place of business. This image shows a rail crane in front of the former Cauble warehouse in 2005. Several pieces of special rail equipment were in Pekin to repair the tracks after a CSX train derailment.

Cauble's Hatchery, Inc.

PEKIN   PHONE 112   INDIANA

VANTRESS CROSS and FIRST GENERATION
ARBOR ACRE WHITE ROCK CHICKS

We have servicemen to help you Broiler Growers, Hog Raisers and Livestock men with your feed programs

MICRO-MIXED
PURINA
BROILER
CHOW

MICRO-MIXED
PURINA
SOW and PIG
CHOW

MICRO-MIXED
PURINA
COW
CHOW

CAUBLE'S HATCHERY. This advertisement, found in a 1955 Washington County Farm Directory, tells of the assistance Cauble's Hatchery, a Monon Railroad vendor, was offering local broiler producers and hog raisers. The broiler industry was an important part of the economy of the Pekin area. The Cauble hatchery was then used as a feed store, a feed-grinding plant, and a mixing plant. (Courtesy of the 1955 Washington County Farm Directory.)

Three

THE MONON IN SALEM

THE FOGG SIDING. This image was taken from the cab of a Monon Railroad C-420 diesel engine by photographer Dick Fontaine. The location is at the Fogg siding, located east of Salem. Another Monon train awaits the passing of the photographer's train. Sidings are instrumental to the safe movement of trains going up and down the tracks simultaneously. (Courtesy of Dick Fontaine.)

TRAIN NO. 72 HEADING NORTH. This image shows Monon Railroad freight train No. 72 heading north from Salem in May 1971. Dave Ritenour took this photograph of the train being pulled by diesel No. 504, a C-420 engine. To the left is the Salem grain elevator, and to the right, south of the tracks, is the O. P. Link Handle Company complex. (Courtesy of Dave Ritenour.)

MONON DEPOT AT SALEM. This Tom Smart photograph shows a passenger train stopped at the depot in October 1964. It was in January 1851 that the first Monon train chugged into Salem. The depot was built in 1909 and used until its closing in 1973 by the Louisville and Nashville Railroad. It was torn down in 1982. In its heyday, the depot was manned by agents, clerks, and telegraphers 24 hours a day. (Courtesy of the MRHTS.)

LINK HANDLE COMPANY WORKERS. The sign above the building tells it all: "America's Finest Handles." The O. P. Link Handle Company made quality hickory handles and took advantage of the availability of huge amounts of hardwood timber found in southern Indiana. As the name implies, O. P. Link was the founder, and his son Norman was manager in the 1970s. (Courtesy of the Stevens Memorial Museum.)

O. P. LINK HANDLE COMPANY. The O. P. Link Handle Company once held the distinction of being the world's largest producer of wooden handles. The company began in 1923 and closed in 2003. In 1990, the company had about 80–85 employees. This image shows the plant yard with partially processed wood and stacks of hickory logs. Link also had factories in three other locations. In 2007, the property was cleared and is now vacant. (Courtesy of the Stevens Memorial Museum.)

53

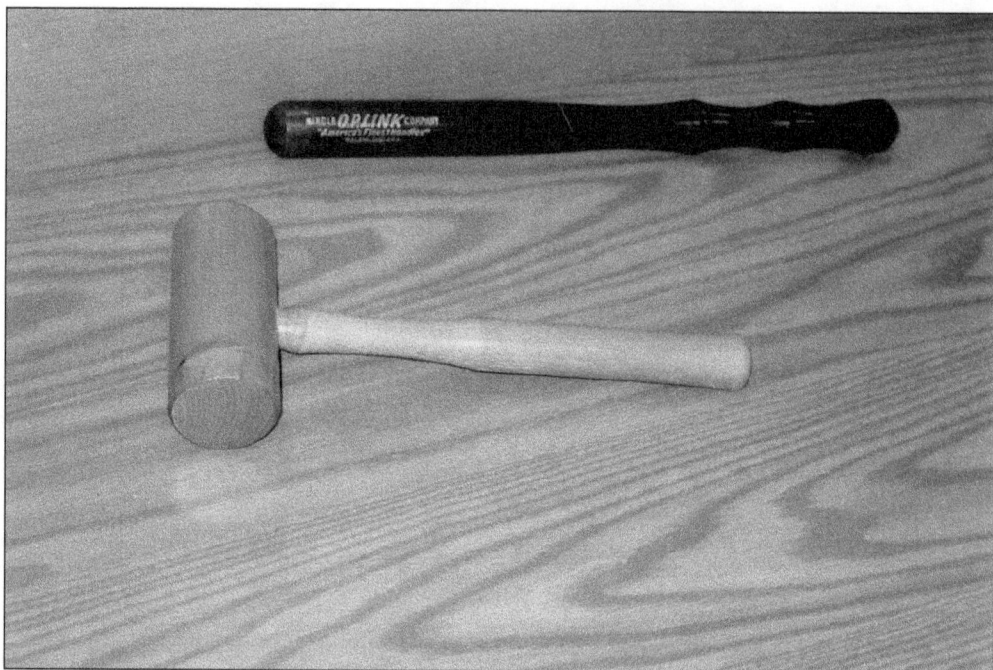

LINK HANDLE COMPANY PRODUCTS. The O. P. Link Handle Company produced the fine handles shown in this photograph. The top item is a billy club made by the Link company. The print on the club says, "America's Finest Handles." The lower handle is that of a wood mallet. The Monon Railroad for many years shipped logs to the plant and picked up the finished product. (Courtesy of the Stevens Memorial Museum.)

SALEM CHEESE AND MILK PLANT. In the 1920s, many in the Salem area desired that the community have a dairy-processing company of its own. On February 22, 1928, area dairy farmers pledged to donate the milk from 1,500 cows to this new cheese operation. In 1980, the Salem Cheese and Milk Company still had 68 employees. This image shows the now-abandoned facility, located on the corner of South Main Street and Old State Road 60.

SMITH CABINET COMPANY. Salem became known for its fine wood products. Smith Cabinet Company began in 1911 and was the Monon Railroad's largest customer in Washington County. This early image shows the Monon rail line in the truly horse-and-buggy days. Smith Cabinet Company was at a time Washington County's largest employer, with about 950 employees in 1990. The company shipped television and radio cabinets nationwide. (Courtesy of the Stevens Memorial Museum.)

SMITH CABINET COMPANY. This more recent image again shows the rail line, but with the addition of the automobile. In the 1970s, Smith Cabinet Company changed its name to Child Craft, which was its brand of infant and juvenile furniture. Its slogan was "the Grown-up Furniture for Children." The Child Craft Company relocated its factory to New Salisbury after extensive flooding from Brock Creek in 2004. (Courtesy of the Stevens Memorial Museum.)

VACATED SMITH CABINET PLANT. In September 2007, Child Craft, in New Salisbury, announced the possible layoffs of most of its workforce by 2009, when its production operations will be shifted to Honduras. This photograph shows the former Child Craft plant in October 2007 as the current business, Trackside Recycling and Warehousing, LLC, was having part of the old plant torn down.

TARR LUMBER CO.

"The House That Service Built" ———— "Where The Customer Is King"
——————————— SPECIALIZING IN ———————————

Commercial & Residential Remodeling

PHONE 601W YOUR LUMBER NUMBER
400 S. Main St.   "SEE US TODAY"   Salem, Ind.

TARR LUMBER COMPANY. The Monon Railroad carried flatcars and boxcars of lumber and other wood products to Tarr Lumber Company in the mid-1950s. Its yard was located at 400 South Main Street. Today the Goodwill store is located on this site. The image shows a couple of Tarr Lumber's spirited slogans. Tarr Lumber advertised the importance of good service and the value of the customer. (Courtesy of the 1955 Washington County Farm Directory.)

FARM BUREAU COMPLEX. For many years, the Washington-Scott County Farm Bureau buildings were a busy stop for the Monon. In the late 1950s, the farm bureau received an average of over 30 train car loads of grain and feed and was an active shipper with the railroad. This image shows one of the former farm bureau co-op feed supply buildings on South Water Street.

Wash-Scott Co. Farm Bureau

CO-OPERATIVE ASSOCIATION, INC.

GRAIN — FEEDS — SEEDS
FARM MACHINERY
— FERTILIZER —

PETROLEUM PRODUCTS
HOME APPLIANCES
BUILDING SUPPLIES
INSECTICIDES, etc.

Farmer Owned . . . Farmer Controlled

STORES LOCATED AT

SALEM	SCOTTSBURG	CAMPBELLSBURG	PEKIN
Phone 295	Phone 2261	Phone 56	Phone 240

WASH-SCOTT COUNTY FARM BUREAU CO-OPERATIVE ASSOCIATION. In 1927, the Pekin and the Salem farm bureaus merged and became the Washington County Farm Bureau Co-op Association. The co-op began handling feed, fertilizer, and fencing and later added petroleum products. Farm Bureau Inc.'s current role is to promote agriculture and help to increase farmers' income by providing information and by lobbying. (Courtesy of the 1955 Washington County Farm Directory.)

WILLIAMS LUMBER AND CONSTRUCTION COMPANY. The Williams Lumber and Construction Company was begun by Paul Williams in 1955. His sons Robert and Richard took the company over upon his death. This lumber company was instrumental in the construction of Salem's Gould Building and the Bata Building. The main buildings and some others structures remain today. At one time a rail siding ran into the property.

KRAFT CHEESE PLANT. This photograph shows the Kraft Cheese plant, located west of Salem, just off Mulberry Street. The railroad siding that the plant used has since been removed. Later it became part of the Salem Cheese and Milk Company plant downtown. It was also used as an onion-processing plant. As trains pass through Salem, it is still to this day referred to as "the cheese plant."

SOUTHBOUND DIESEL APPROACHES SALEM. An INRD train runs by a lumber mill west of Salem. This mill has no siding and uses trucks to deliver logs and to transport its product. In June 2006, the INDR obtained trackage rights from the Canadian Pacific Railway for trackage from Terre Haute to Bedford. Previously acquired trackage rights had given the INRD trackage from Bedford, milepost (MP) 246 south to Louisville, on the old Monon Railroad tracks.

HITCHCOCK FLAG STOP. This photograph shows the building at Hitchcock, just north of Salem, that served the Monon as a flag stop. If flagged, the train would stop at such privately owned businesses to pick up passengers or drop them off. Farabee, just north of Pekin, and Harristown were also Monon flag stops. This photograph was taken in 2000, not long before the structure was demolished. (Courtesy of Cecil Smith.)

CAMPBELLSBURG FARM BUREAU GRAIN ELEVATOR. Campbellsburg was first called Buena Vista, which was named for a battle in the Mexican War. It was platted in 1849 and named for Robert Campbell. It is a small town located north of Salem in an agrarian community. For many years, Campbellsburg had a depot, and this grain elevator was quite active in the fall months. The depot was torn down in 1962.

DIESEL PASSES THROUGH CAMPBELLSBURG. This photograph shows an INDR train passing through Campbellsburg in the fall of 2007. To the left of the train is the grain elevator that used to operate here. The facility is now used by local businessman David Lee, who purchased the Campbellsburg elevator to use the structures for farm storage. Campbellsburg once was a regular stop on the Monon timetable.

Four

THE MONON IN
ORLEANS AND WEST

MONON DEPOT AT ORLEANS. Orleans was once known as a railroad town. That statement was evidenced when the town citizens raised $40,000 of private subscription to secure the Monon Railroad coming there in the winter of 1851–1852. This image shows the most recent Orleans depot with the familiar Monon sign hanging over the door. It was built in 1898 at a cost of just over $16,000. Around 1946, the depot was remodeled and shortened. (Courtesy of the Dick Fontaine.)

APPROACHING ORLEANS DEPOT. This image, taken in May 1971, shows the depot without the waiting area. In its heyday, Orleans may have seen as many as 22 trains daily stopping at the depot. For many travelers, Orleans was a layover; they used the restaurants, newsstand, and hotels. The Louisville and Nashville Railroad closed the depot in 1973. At one time, trains could run through the depot like the depot at Gosport. (Courtesy of Dave Ritenour.)

ORLEANS GOODRICH GRAIN AND FEED. This image shows the Orleans Goodrich Grain and Feed elevator, built in 1920. In its beginning, farmers brought grain to the elevator by wagon or by rail. Workers weighed, sorted, and shipped the grain to a larger terminal elevator where the grains could be distributed to local, national, or international markets. Today trucks have replaced the railroad in collecting and hauling the area's grain.

ORLEANS MAID DAIRY. This photograph shows the Orleans Maid Dairy building, built in 1920 for the Producers Marketing Association. Its purpose was to organize and promote the marketing of local dairy products to the benefit of the local dairy farmers. The building is located on Maple Street and is locally referred to as the "refrigerated building."

ORANGE COUNTY CONCRETE COMPANY. In the late 1950s, the Orange County Concrete Company received over 90 railcars of sand, cement, and gravel by way of the Monon Railroad. The business has changed ownership over the years but has still kept the original name. Located on Jefferson Street, the plant was in view of the depot and the curved track through town.

TRAV-LER RADIO CORPORATION. This plant site, in the northeast part of Orleans, is located where the Orleans Cabinet Company was first located. When Orleans Cabinet moved to Paoli, its name was changed to the Paoli Chair Company. The buildings shown here were used by the Trav-Ler Radio Corporation, producers of radios and televisions. More recently it was used by Admiral, United Technologies, and Essex International. Today it is used by Seed America.

WHEELER-FOUTCH COMPANY. The Wheeler-Foutch Company was in the dry goods and grocery business. It also had businesses in Bedford and Leipsic. It was still receiving goods by Monon rail delivery in the late 1950s. Its building still stands along the former Monon tracks. The building has had several uses since Wheeler-Foutch vacated, including use as a venue for country music.

THE STETSON HOUSE. This home, also called the Shindler House, a Philadelphia-style house, was a gift to the parents of Sarah Shindler. Sarah was born in 1858 in Orleans and was extremely talented musically. She was heard singing in Philadelphia by John Stetson, wealthy widower and hat manufacturer, while she was visiting there with an uncle. At their meeting, she was 20 and he was 48. Romance developed, and six years later they married. In 1894, after the marriage, Stetson came to Orleans and bought Sarah's parents a 430-acre farm. He then had this two-story, Philadelphia-style, prefabricated house sent to them. The house was delivered unassembled on Monon railcars, and Stetson sent his workmen to then construct the house. Locally it is referred to by both names, the Stetson House and the Shindler House. It is located at 630 Washington Street.

CRAWFORD-MORRIS LUMBER COMPANY. The roots of this business began in Mitchell in 1901 when Henry Crawford purchased a lumberyard there. He died in 1937, and a partnership began between the Crawford heirs and Raymond Morris. The property in the photograph was acquired by the Crawford-Morris Lumber Company in 1946. In the 1950s, Crawford-Morris Lumber Company received building materials by way of the Monon Railroad.

PAOLI DEPOT. This image is of the Paoli combination depot. The depot was used for freight and passengers and was demolished in the 1970s, after the Monon merger with the Louisville and Nashville Railroad. The Louisville and Nashville Railroad ended the rail stop at French Lick in 1976, leaving the stop in Paoli the last on the branch. (Courtesy of the MRHTS.)

THE PAOLI TRESTLE. The initial Paoli trestle was constructed of wood and built north of Paoli. It was a curved bridge that was nearly 1,400 feet long and 75 feet high. In just over 10 years of use, it was abandoned because of safety concerns as wooden bridges had a poor reputation because of their collapsing or catching fire. This image shows its steel replacement. (Courtesy of Dick Fontaine.)

STEAM ON THE STEEL TRESTLE. This photograph shows a steam locomotive pulling a Monon passenger train on the Paoli trestle. The trestle was one of the more unusual attractions for those passengers crossing the valley and heading for a relaxing stay at West Baden or French Lick. (Courtesy of Larry Pritchett.)

PAOLI STEEL BRIDGE. Steel and precast concrete soon replaced wood in the building of railroad trestles. The old wooden Paoli trestle was taken down in 1904; it was replaced with a new steel bridge at a cost of $120,000. It spanned 870 feet and was 85 feet high. Two stone abutments were at each end, and there were 36 stone bases between the span on which the trestle framing sat. In this new design, the architect added small open-ended boxes for workers who may have to seek refuge in the event that a train would cross unexpectedly. The 80-year-old Monon Railroad trestle was razed in July 1982, as the Louisville and Nashville Railroad abandoned the tracks from Paoli to Orleans. Crewmen began disassembly by removing crossties from the trestle. This photograph was taken during the dismantling process. Today all that remains are the north- and south-end bridge abutments. (Courtesy of Jim Craig.)

MONON TRAIN CREW. It is the job of the train crew to move trains and make sure that the customers' freight gets delivered safely and expediently. In actuality, many of the railroad jobs were hard, dirty, and on occasion dangerous. The jobs within a traditional train crew might include engineer, fireman, conductor, station agent, yardmaster, clerk, and brakeman. These workers were often away from home and worked irregular hours. These jobs may lead to a worker becoming a conductor or a locomotive engineer, where one would have an opportunity to work onboard a moving locomotive. The conductor is responsible for the train, the freight, and the crew while the engineer operates the engine. This locomotive, an NW-2, was delivered to the Monon in 1946. From left to right, behind the handrail are Marion "Ike" Cunningham (engineer), Fred Franks, Bill Wagner, Bill Clay, and Bud Lee. (Courtesy of Larry Pritchett.)

MONON SECTION CREW. Many railroad companies divided the tracks into sections, but the amount of track that they were responsible for varied since the number of auxiliary tracks also varied. Each section was usually assigned a foreman and crew. The size of the crews also varied, and the size became less over the years, as new equipment would replace the number of workers needed in the crew. Likewise, the numbers of crews needed also diminished. The section crew's main jobs included track maintenance, which included installing ties, replacing broken rails, tamping ballast under low track joints and at road crossings, and mowing the railroad's right-of-way. This image shows a Monon Railroad section crew and some tools used. From left to right are (first row) section foreman Claude Pritchett, Reed Roll, John Phillips, Frank Taylor, and Bill Dean; (second row) Joe Wells and Steven Jones. (Courtesy of Larry Pritchett.)

INDIANA HANDLE COMPANY. The Indiana Handle Company, established in 1922, employs about 140 workers. It is located at 1514 West Main Street, west of Paoli on U.S. Highway 50. The plant produces wood furniture turnings for sporting equipment and furniture legs. The plant also is the nation's third-leading producer of croquet mallets, making over 70,000 croquet sets annually.

INDIANA HANDLE COMPANY PLANT. The Monon Railroad tracks were along the hillside and north of the Indiana Handle Company. These tracks continued west to West Baden and French Lick. This image shows some of the buildings and structures that belong to the Indiana Handle Company. To the east of the plant was where the Cornwell Company plant was located before it was destroyed by fire in January 1974.

TRAIN WRECK IN PAOLI. As Larry Pritchett was growing up, he had a few adventures others may not have. His father and two grandfathers worked for the Monon Railroad, gaining him some access to happenings such as this 1947 Monon freight train derailment behind the Indiana Handle Company. From left to right are Larry Pritchett with his grandfather Claude Pritchett. (Courtesy of Larry Pritchett.)

KNOX-HUTCHINS FURNITURE COMPANY. In 1903, Sam Knox, Charles Denny, and Alvis Wells started a furniture company named the Paoli Cabinet Company. This company was incorporated in 1906 and was also producing cabinets and tables. In 1917, the Knox-Hutchins Furniture Company was formed, and M. W. Hutchins, of Chicago, was the new vice president. The plant shown in this photograph was located on Third Street in Paoli. (Courtesy of the Orange County Historical Society.)

72

PAOLI CHAIR COMPANY. Business slowed for the Knox-Hutchins Furniture Company in the 1920s while the Orleans Cabinet Company was busy producing chairs and dining room and bedroom furniture. The Orleans Cabinet Company borrowed money for expansion from New Albany's American Bank, which proved to be a poor decision, as it soon went into receivership. Paoli Chair Company then operated Orleans Cabinet Company until it closed in 1926. (Courtesy of Tom Rankin.)

CHAIR COMPANY WORKERS. American Bank's Sam Elsby reopened the Orleans Cabinet Company in 1928, making Frank McCracken the manager. McCracken operated both the Paoli and Orleans plants until 1931, when the Orleans plant closed and Paoli Chair continued in Paoli. This is why the Paoli Chair Company is said to have been begun in Orleans. In 1995, Paoli Furniture moved to Orleans. This image shows Paoli Chair Company workers in front of a CI&L boxcar. (Courtesy of the Orange County Historical Society.)

KRAFT FOODS PLANT. Paoli's Kraft Foods Company was located near the Paoli Chair Company plant and on the east side of the Monon Railroad tracks. The factory made natural cheese products and utilized boxcars. By the late 1950s, the Monon was not making deliveries at the plant but the plant did ship some of its products by boxcar. (Courtesy of Terry Cornwell.)

TOMATO PRODUCTS COMPANY. This photograph shows the Tomato Products Company complex. The factory was located above the Monon rail line, above where the Farlow Lumber Company was located. This image shows the two main buildings, the water tank, and a steam locomotive on the siding. The tomato plant burned in the 1940s. (Courtesy of Ken Weller.)

TOMATO PRODUCTS PLANT. The remains of the Tomato Products plant can be seen from an access road off West Fourth Street. It has been altered as buildings were removed and additions were made. Tomato plants were seasonal and often had no more than 10 to 12 workers. The foundations of the other structures and the railroad siding bed can still be located on the property.

FARLOW LUMBER COMPANY. Moulder Farlow acquired the Studebaker sawmill in 1885, and this later became the Farlow Lumber Company. His son, Paul, later owned the lumber company. While growing up, Paul would help his father, Moulder, drive oxen teams pulling loads of logs to the Monon depot in Orleans or to the Studebaker plant in Paoli. Studebaker made wagon parts, which were sent to South Bend for assembly. The structures shown in this photograph were once part of the Farlow Lumber Company.

MONON BRIDGE AT ABYDEL. One of the few remaining Monon Railroad bridges in southern Indiana is still standing west of Paoli on U.S. Highway 150 at Abydel. The steel girders and rails to the left of the stone abutment have been removed, and the paint showing the Monon symbols has nearly faded away. Over the years, this small bridge carried many tourists from many parts of Indiana into the mineral springs resorts at West Baden and French Lick. (Courtesy of Jim Craig.)

WEST BADEN PASSENGER DEPOT. This depot has been torn down since the 1970s. Wealthy travelers from Louisville, Chicago, Indianapolis, and Cincinnati routinely made their way to West Baden via the Monon Railroad. On the first Saturdays in May, the Kentucky Derby brought hoards of visitors to West Baden and French Lick, as this was a rather short commute to Churchill Downs in Louisville. Monon Railroad records show that the stone depot with its tile roof was built at West Baden in 1906 for $21,222. (Courtesy of the MRHTS.)

WEST BADEN SPRINGS HOTEL. The first hotel in West Baden was built in 1852, several years before the Monon Railroad extended its rails from Paoli to West Baden in 1887. After the Monon had completed rail construction to the springs areas, both the French Lick and West Baden inns built large additions. In 1888, Lee Sinclair bought controlling interest in the West Baden Springs Hotel and made several major improvements. A casino and an opera house were added to the West Baden grounds. Although the Monon Railroad certainly promoted tourism, tourism was never more than marginally lucrative for the railroad. The present resort hotel at West Baden was built in 1902, after fire in 1901 destroyed the resort. The new hotel with the huge dome operated until 1932 when the effects of the 1929 depression were more than the hotel could overcome. This image was taken in 1922 and shows the resort's original spires. (Courtesy of the New Albany-Floyd County Public Library.)

WEST BADEN SPRINGS HOTEL AND ATRIUM. After the 1929 stock market crash, the hotel was finished, and owner Charles Ballard was unable to sell the resort. He decided to give the inn to the Society of Jesus, the Jesuits, and it became its seminary in 1933. In 1966, the property became a regional campus of Northwood Institute. In 1983, the property became vacant and remained so until 1996. That was when entrepreneur Bill Cook and his wife, Gayle, of Bloomington financed a partial restoration of the hotel by the Historic Landmarks Foundation of Indiana, which held the title. Over 400,000 people were drawn to the hotel to see the 135-foot-high atrium and the other highlights of the property over the next decade. On October 24, 1998, Erickson Air Crane, of Nebraska, brought *Bubba*, a huge helicopter, to lift and set the four redesigned spires in place. The reconstruction of the four spires seemed to set the mood for other improvements to come. (Courtesy of Dick Fontaine.)

WEST BADEN RESORT. In 2006, the title to the West Baden Springs Hotel was transferred to Bill Cook's Cook Group, and the full restoration began. It was completed in the spring of 2007. This image shows the resort as it looks today. Several million dollars have been spent on the refurbishing of the resort to bring it back to the grandeur that it was in its beginning. The refurbished hotel opened in the spring of 2007, and the hotel began filling up the 246 luxury rooms. It is a striking piece of architecture, and there is nothing like it in the Midwest. The dome was the United States' largest free-spanning atrium until the Houston Dome was constructed in the 1960s. This photograph shows the resort with the four corner spires in place. The original spires had been removed several years ago, but new copies of the original ones were produced and installed in 1998.

WEST BADEN PATRONS. This posed photograph was taken on the lawn of the West Baden Springs Hotel by photographer J. C. Stewart. People came to the West Baden and French Lick for the springwaters, the spas, and the health regiment they offered. There were three different springwaters used by the inns, and some were even mixed together to gain a certain balance for bodily fluid elimination. (Courtesy of the New Albany-Floyd County Public Library.)

FRENCH LICK PASSENGER STATION. The depot at French Lick was built in 1907 at a cost of $20,606. The juncture depot's usage was shared for many years with the Southern Railway. This limestone station has been home to the Indiana Railway Museum since 1978. This photograph shows the back of the depot and a passenger train sitting on the trackside. The French Lick and West Baden and Southern Tourist Railroad (FLWB&S) offers excellent rail excursions for the railfan.

"The Home of Pluto Water"

French Lick Springs Hotel, French Lick, Ind.

FRENCH LICK SPRINGS HOTEL. French Lick grew out of the popularity of the local springwater. French Lick got its name from the early French settlers and the local mineral licks used by area wildlife. The French Lick Springs Hotel, shown in this old postcard, was noted for its sports facilities, spas, and baths. A 2006 face-lift has returned the French Lick Springs Hotel to the stately beauty of the 1920s. (Courtesy of C. T. American Art Postcards.)

For a Glorious Fall Vacation!

FRENCH LICK SPRINGS
AMERICA'S FAVORITE SPA

Plan now to spend your fall vacation on this 2000 acre "country estate". Autumn is the perfect time to enjoy the exceptional sports facilities, the social activities, and a "pick-up" in vitality afforded by the famed therapeutic baths and mineral waters. Excellent cuisine, new cocktail lounge, dancing.
TWO CHAMPIONSHIP GOLF COURSES • RIDING • ARCHERY
TENNIS • BADMINTON • HIKING • SKEET SHOOTING
Served by Monon and B & O Railroads—Private Airport

FRENCH LICK SPRINGS HOTEL

Home of Pluto Water
FRENCH LICK, INDIANA
MICHAEL J. KELLEY, GENERAL MANAGER

CHICAGO
522 S. Michigan Avenue
WAbash 9045-46

NEW YORK
11 W. 42nd Street
BRyant 9-6347

WASHINGTON
1430 F. Street, N. W.
EXecutive 6481

FRENCH LICK SPRINGS HOTEL ADVERTISEMENT. This advertisement was used in a 1947 Monon Railroad centennial booklet to promote the French Lick resort. It was the place to be for sports, social activities, and the therapy that the mineral waters and spas could bring patrons. Its advertisement also mentioned that the Monon Railroad and Baltimore and Ohio Railroad could bring one to this enjoyable destination. (Courtesy of Monon Centennial Booklet.)

FRENCH LICK FREIGHT HOUSE. The French Lick freight house is still standing and can be found by walking about a quarter of a mile north of the passenger depot. It was built in 1929 and is now used by the FLWB&S for maintaining the trackage, equipment, and structures. This photograph shows the French Lick train yard in 1932. (Courtesy of the MRHTS.)

PLUTO WATER BOTTLING HOUSE. This image shows the Pluto bottling plant located directly across from the French Lick resort. Pluto water has been called "America's Physic" and was a huge part of the draw that brought travelers to the valley. Today the draw that brings tourists to French Lick is the gaming boat located in front of the resort.

Five

THE MONON IN BEDFORD

MITCHELL MONON DEPOT. Built in 1892, the Mitchell Monon Railroad depot was torn down in the 1970s. The depot was an important part of the Monon line, and with the junction of the Baltimore and Ohio Railroad, Mitchell was quite busy. The 23,000-square-foot depot was of frame construction and cost only $4,304 to construct. At one time, there were three other railroad buildings at the site. (Courtesy of the MRHTS, Charles Huffer Collection.)

LEHIGH PORTLAND CEMENT COMPANY. Lehigh Cement had its beginning in Allentown, Pennsylvania, in 1897. In 1902, a large deposit of limestone was purchased in Mitchell by Lehigh. The plant shown in this postcard was erected in Mitchell the same year. Immigrant workers from Romania, Serbia, Greece, and Hungary were employed when the plant first opened. This postcard has a postmark reflecting the year 1953 and shows only a portion of the huge plant. (Courtesy of Commercial Chrome Postcards.)

LEHIGH CEMENT BAGS. Lehigh Cement Company was the major industry in Mitchell from its beginning. Lehigh produces gray, white, and custom colored and blended cements. It also produces aggregates, ready-mix concrete, block, and other related construction materials. This photograph shows Clarence Robinson, an employee of New Albany's L. Thorn Company, moving a palate of Lehigh Cement bags. (Courtesy of Bill Hacker.)

THE LEHIGH PLANT WORKERS. The Lehigh plant is located on the east side of Mitchell. This image shows a group of quarry workers several years ago, sitting in front of the stone quarry. Among the quarry workers are Arelus White (first row, second from left), Claude White (first row, far right), and Laurence Ellis (standing). (Courtesy of Charlie White.)

MONON CLOSED HOPPER CARS. This photograph was taken on September 29, 1984, several years after the merger and end of the Monon Railroad. It shows three loaded covered hopper cars, No. 52048, No. 52025, and No. 52077, sitting on the Monon siding east of Mitchell alongside the Lehigh Portland Cement Company plant, waiting for delivery. From 1958 to 1960, the Monon delivered to Lehigh an average of 260 train cars of raw materials annually. (Courtesy of George Lortz.)

LEHIGH PLANT SWITCH ENGINE. In the late 1950s, the Monon Railroad shipped an average of over 600 cement train cars per year from the Lehigh plant. This image shows the switch engine that Lehigh used to move railcars throughout the plant complex. Today trucks are constantly seen in and around the Lehigh plant and they no longer use the railroad to ship their products. (Courtesy of Jim Craig.)

ROBERTS BRASS COMPANY. This structure was once the home of the Roberts Brass Company, which came to Mitchell in the early 1950s. In the late 1950s, the Monon delivered an average of about 10 railcars of materials annually. Roberts produced air cocks, steam gauge cocks, and water gauges. It also made small brass valves and fittings for the gas appliance industry. It sold its products nationally and employed more than 150 workers.

MITCHELL FEED AND GRAIN. Mitchell Feed and Grain was used mostly by the Baltimore and Ohio Railroad in Mitchell. However, it may have been used as part of the Monon team track for some deliveries. This image does give an excellent view the Monon main line looking south, in Mitchell. This image was taken in May 1971. (Courtesy of Dave Ritenour.)

FREIGHT TRAIN AT MITCHELL. This photograph shows a southbound Canadian Pacific Railway freight train at Mitchell in April 2006. The image shows what had been the Monon and Baltimore and Ohio crossing diamond. The Canadian Pacific train is headed by engine No. 9728. Today CSX and Indiana Railroad trains are also seen on the old Monon line. (Courtesy of Jim Craig.)

PASSENGERS AT BEDFORD. The New Albany and Salem Railroad, later called the Monon Railroad, first arrived in Bedford in 1853. Some of the earlier depot agents at Bedford included M. J. Edgeworth and H. P. Radley. This image, taken around 1964, shows the Bedford passenger depot as passengers are unloading Monon train No. 6. This depot is now being used as a community recycling center. (Courtesy of the MRHTS, Charles Huffer Collection.)

MONON DEPOT AT BEDFORD. Without the railroad, the heavy limestone blocks quarried in the area could not have been transported and the limestone industry could not have developed as it did. The construction of public buildings using limestone became popular because of its beauty and strength. This image shows the Bedford passenger depot, which was constructed in 1926 of Indiana limestone. (Courtesy of the MRHTS, Charles Huffer Collection.)

BEDFORD FREIGHT HOUSE. In 1971, the Monon merged into the Louisville and Nashville Railroad. This image shows a Louisville and Nashville Railroad diesel in front of the Monon freight house in May 1976. The Louisville and Nashville Railroad became a familiar sight, but to many it did not take the place of Indiana's own Monon. (Courtesy of Jim Craig.)

LIMESTONE BRIDGE SUPPORTS. One of the early uses for Indiana limestone was for road and railroad bridge abutments. This image shows limestone abutment piers under the Monon railroad bridge above the Wildcat River near Frankfort, Indiana. Rail and road bridges across Indiana can be found with similar limestone supports. (Courtesy of the Lawrence County Museum, Frank Fish Collection.)

QUARRYING LIMESTONE. Lawrence County first began quarrying limestone in the 1830s. The earliest acquisition of stone was to simply gather what nature had left broken or freed in various places. Later workers tried to create ways to remove stone from places where the stone had been deposited nearer to the surface. In time, star drills were used by quarrymen to drill horizontally and vertically into the rock. Then black powder was filled in the holes to blast the drill-loosened block from the cliff and onto the quarry floor below. In 1875, a steam-powered channeling machine was brought from Vermont to the Bedford area by John Matthews of Matthews Brothers Stone Company of Ellettsville. By 1890, the stone belt had 35 Wardwell channelers in use. This image shows several channeling machines in an Oolitic quarry, north of Bedford. (Courtesy of Steve Stafford.)

BLASTING STONE AT DOYLE QUARRY. This image shows several steam-powered channeling machines at the Doyle Quarry near Bedford. The channeling machine was basically a steam locomotive running on steel rails that had been attached to the quarry floor. The driving device had long-shafted chisels attached to it, and these chisels impacted with the stone in a line parallel to the rail itself. The channels ran vertically and horizontally and then intersected to free the block on four sides. Wedges were then used to break loose certain blocks along the bottom. When these were broken free, the blocks could then be lifted out of the hole. Often the break in the block was not in the place desired, and further drilling would then occur to reach the quarry floor. On the quarry floor where the blocks will fall, one can see many small broken fragments of stone called spalls. These are left intentionally to help absorb and cushion the fall of the blocks. (Courtesy of the Lawrence County Museum, Frank Fish Collection.)

MONON RAIL GONDOLAS. Before the appearance of railroads, stone blocks were moved on high-wheeled oxen carts. Transporting the blocks was quite dangerous and laborious for the workers. The derricks were used to lift the blocks out of the hole and onto railroad gondola cars. This photograph shows Monon Railroad gondolas No. 31163 and No. 31409 at the Dark Hollow Quarry near Bedford in the 1930s. (Courtesy of the Lawrence County Museum, Frank Fish Collection.)

BLACK DIAMOND MILL. CI&L flatcar No. 627 is shown in this photograph at the Black Diamond Mill near Bedford. Painted above the flatcar identification are the words "Quarry to Mill." This would help the switcher to know that this car was not to leave the quarry property and that this car was destined to go to the mill for the stone to be cut as ordered. (Courtesy of the Lawrence County Museum.)

DARK HOLLOW QUARRY. This image gives a good look at the track system on which the steam channeling machines ran. Within the quarry are four channeling machines belching black smoke. Several workers can be seen working within the quarry. CI&L gondola No. 4041 and a CI&L flatcar are seen to the far left, at gray hole, ledge B of Dark Hollow Quarry. (Courtesy of the Lawrence County Museum, Frank Fish Collection.)

QUARRY AT OOLITIC. This photograph was taken at the Perry, Mathews, and Buskirk (PM&B) quarry at Oolitic. In the photograph are three or four loaded gondolas, one of which is a Monon gondola. The photograph was taken in 1955. Oolitic is a few miles north of Bedford and today is home of the Indiana Limestone Company. (Courtesy of Tim Swan.)

CHANNELING OPERATION. This image shows a close-up of a steam channeling machine, accompanied by two quarry workers. The man on the left is standing directly above what appears to be a cut in the stone, made by the machine. This may have been an image taken for the purposes of demonstrating the company's operations in the quarry for sales or instruction. (Courtesy of the Lawrence County Museum.)

MONON STEAM LOCOMOTIVE. This image was taken in 1931 and shows Monon Railroad steam locomotive No. 121 in Bedford. In the background is the Shea and Donnelly Limestone Mill. The limestone mill takes the limestone block and reduces it to the particular shapes and cuts that are ordered. This Monon steam engine was purchased in 1923. This photograph was taken at the Monon Bedford and Bloomfield (B&B) engine facility. (Courtesy of the MRHTS.)

FLUTED COLUMNS. This image shows a fluted limestone column loaded on a Monon flatcar. A special milling attachment is used to complete the fluting, and the lathe can hold columns up to 35 feet in length. Great care was taken to protect such detailed, specialized carving. Under each strap, blocks were used to keep the strapping from causing damage to the fluting. (Courtesy of the Lawrence County Museum, Walter Long Collection.)

FLATCARS OF LIMESTONE COLUMNS. This photograph shows two rail spurs, each loaded with limestone columns. The stone on these flatcars was lathe turned at the Doyle Stone Company mill after the stone had been mined at the Dark Hollow Quarry. The Dark Hollow Quarry and the PM&B quarry were regularly scheduled yard engine assignments. (Courtesy of the Lawrence County Museum, Walter Long Collection.)

INDIANA LIMESTONE COMPANY. In 1926, 24 limestone companies and 36 limestone mills merged into the Indiana Limestone Company. This unification of companies greatly benefited the stone industry. This postcard shows the stockpile of huge limestone blocks at the Indiana Limestone Company property at the north edge of Oolitic. The water reservoir shown in the photograph is at the Walsh quarry. (Courtesy of the Johnson Wholesale Company.)

CARBORUNDUM MACHINE. This machine is designed to put a finely ground finish, or a carborundum finish, on limestone that has been cut. This carborundum machine was at the Dickerson Mill. In contrast, a finish can also need an even finer finish or honed finish. A honed finish would be used in a situation that requires the look of a polished surface. (Courtesy of the Lawrence County Museum, Frank Fish Collection.)

TURNING LIMESTONE COLUMNS. The turning of the stone on the lathe is used to create the basic column shape. Rough stone blocks with diameters up to five feet can be turned on such lathes. Lathes like the one in the image can hold blocks weighing 70–80 tons. (Courtesy of the Lawrence County Museum, Walter Long Collection.)

SAWING LIMESTONE. Limestone saws may turn at velocities around 700 revolutions per minute. The sawyer operates the saw, checking and rechecking for precision cuts. The stream of water to the left of the saw is used to reduce friction and improve the cuts. (Courtesy of the Lawrence County Museum, Walter Long Collection.)

LIMESTONE MILL OPERATION. This image shows various activities that occur within a limestone mill. In the foreground are various sizes of cut limestone slabs. In the background is a crew moving a large stone block into place for a cut. The block is being lifted by a ceiling crane with the slab held by cables with workers guiding the load. (Courtesy of the Lawrence County Museum, Frank Fish Collection.)

McGRATH MILL. McGrath Mill was one of many mills operated by the Indiana Limestone Company. This postcard shows the interior of the stone mill, located east of the Monon Railroad tracks on J Street. Mills like this prepared the building material for use in schools, skyscrapers, churches, private homes, and other constructions. Orders also went through these stone mills for fine, artistic, hand-carved statues. (Courtesy of C. T. Art Colortone.)

INDIANA STEEL AND ENGINEERING CORPORATION. The McGrath Mill building was used by McGrath from 1923 to 1961, when it was sold to the Yuba Company. The Indiana Steel and Engineering Corporation began using the structure in 1963. The owner, Joe Elliott, said that his great-grandfather designed some of the Bedford gang saws that are in use today. The company fabricates steel bridges, overhead cranes, and other special-order steelwork. (Courtesy of Jim Craig.)

INGALLS STONE MILL. This photograph shows the mill building used by the Ingalls Stone Company. In 1958, the Monon brought nearly 30 cars to the quarry. In the same year, Ingalls shipped nearly 60 railcars with the Monon Railroad. The number of cars received and shipped diminished greatly by 1960. This image was taken in May 1986. (Courtesy of Jim Craig.)

STEAM CHANNELING MACHINE. This steam channeling machine is on display at one of the Oolitic school campuses. It was used a few years ago for a community function in which the machine's work history was celebrated. An early channeling machine cost quarry owner John Matthews $6,000. By 1890, the Indiana Manufacturing Company of New Albany was producing double gang channelers and selling them for $2,000.

ANGELA STONE COMPANY. This image captured Greg May, Angela Stone Company carver, using a pneumatic carving tool to scroll this soon-to-be decorative limestone piece. Such work years ago was done with hand-carving tools. Today they use air pressure–powered cutting tools. May worked through a four-year apprentice program to attain these skills.

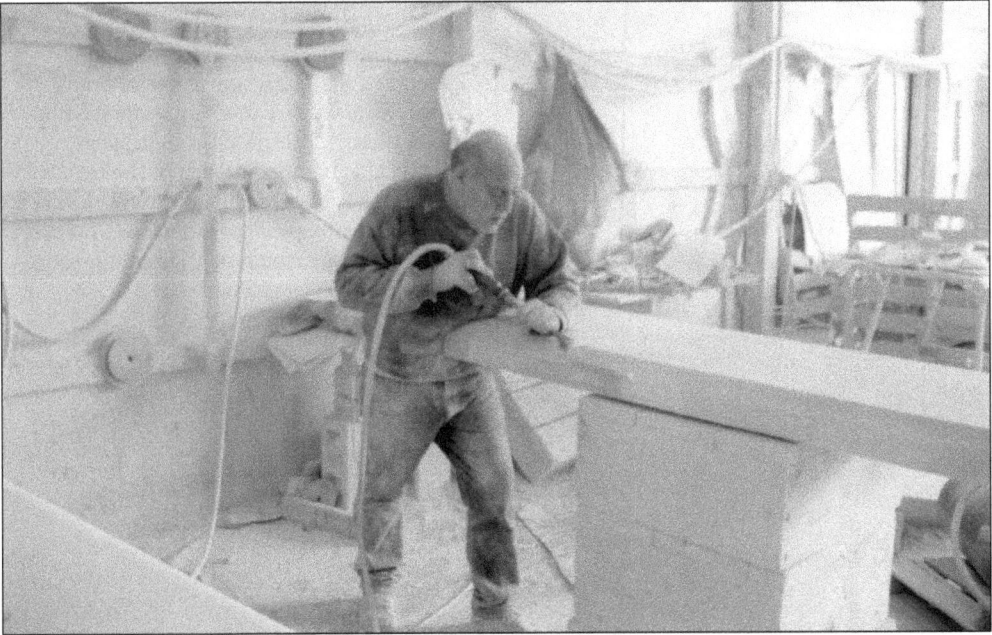

LIMESTONE EDGING TOOL. This carver, also employed by the Angela Stone Company, is trimming the edge of this stone block. This particular cutting tool has a wide point that works in a straight cut, unlike the previous tool that cuts within spiral designs. A finishing blade would be needed to put the final smooth edge on the stone.

THE STONE MILL SAWYER. The sawyer, seen here, had used a forklift to move the limestone beam to the saw area. He then set the beam onto the slats before he began to measure. He checked his measurements several times before climbing up the control area. The entire operation around this particular saw was performed by one worker.

TOOLS OF A STONE CARVER. This monument, at Bedford's Green Hill Cemetery, marks the grave site of Louis Baker, a carver at Rowe's Limestone Mill. Baker died in 1917, and his colleagues created this detailed replica of the bench at which he labored. The entire work was made from one piece of limestone and even shows Baker's name scratched on his tools and cracks in the grained wood.

TREE STUMP CARVINGS. Somewhat common in Green Hill Cemetery are carved tree trunks as in this photograph. The fine detail used to show the trunk itself is impressive. The intricate work in forming the vine encircling the tree trunk is outstanding. The Bedford area had several carvers that were noted for their ability to carve tree trunks.

INDIANA LIMESTONE INSTITUTE OF AMERICA. This limestone building was first used by the Indiana Limestone Institute of America. The institute was created in 1928 to promote, educate, provide technical expertise, and work as an advocate for the Indiana limestone industry. Today the building is used by Oakland City University as a regional campus in Bedford. The building is on J Street.

RELIANCE MANUFACTURING. This image shows the Reliance Manufacturing plant, and the photograph may have been taken from inside the engine. The Reliance Manufacturing Company made shirts. The building is still standing and in use today. Reliance's spur was extended from the Monon Railroad team track from behind the Monon freight house where it crosses at Twelfth Street. (Courtesy of the Lawrence County Museum.)

LANZ LUMBER COMPANY. Lanz Lumber Company was a customer of the Monon Railroad, and Lanz had a spur off the Monon freight house. The lumber company was at the corner of J Street and Fourteenth Street, and this image shows the Monon tracks looking north, toward the depot. The structure was previously used as an opera house. A fire later destroyed the building. (Courtesy of the Lawrence County Museum, Walter Long Collection.)

FABRICAST PLANT. The Monon also did business with the Fabricast plant, a division of General Motors. This current image shows the main business offices for General Motors. The Bedford Foundry has been in operation since 1942. It produces automobile transmission casings. In the late 1950s, the plant received an average of over 180 shipments of sand annually from the Monon Railroad.

BUCK LEMON FURNITURE COMPANY. The Buck Lemon Furniture Company was not a huge customer of the Monon Railroad in the late 1950s. It did receive an average of three train cars of furniture annually during those years and may have received even more in previous years. The building today has been restored and is a currently used as the Lawrence County Museum and has a wealth of information and knowledgeable volunteers.

BEDFORD TRAIN YARD. The Monon Railroad train yard was located north of the passenger depot, near the 246-mile marker. The yard has a capacity of 81 cars, and the passing track could hold 78 cars. The B&B main line was directly west of the Bedford yard. This image was taken in 1932. (Courtesy of the MRHTS.)

FLATBED TRUCKS LOADED WITH STONE. Railroads no longer run into the limestone quarries, nor do they transport the large cut blocks from the quarry to the mill. Trucks such as these are used to haul cut stone from the mill and deliver it to the customers. These trucks were found loaded at the Evans Limestone Company mill. The Evans Limestone Company has been in business since 1958.

SALT CREEK BRIDGE. In this image, a Monon Railroad C-420 diesel cab was used as a good vantage to photograph the Middle Salt Creek Bridge located between Murdock and Harrodsburg, just south of Guthrie. Guthrie is located north of Bedford at mile marker No. 235. (Courtesy of Dick Fontaine.)

NORTHBOUND LOCAL AT GUTHRIE. Photographer Dick Fontaine caught the northbound local coming through Guthrie on July 31, 1971. This was just weeks before the Monon Railroad merged with the Louisville and Nashville Railroad. Longtime Monon employee Mahlon "Cookie" Eberhard was caught waving at this freight, the next to the last Monon train on the south end. (Courtesy of Dick Fontaine.)

BEDFORD TRAIN SHED. Railroads have always been concerned with mechanical problems, track hazards, and other safety dangers. This image shows a Bedford train shed that was used by car inspectors. It was their job to visually look for and anticipate problems that may occur. Today advances in technology can detect most of these concerns. (Courtesy of Dick Fontaine.)

BEDFORD RAIL BRIDGE. This railroad bridge was located on the old B&B branch west of Bedford. The B&B had about 45 miles of three-foot narrow-gauge track and was acquired by the Monon Railroad in 1886. Its trackage went northwest of Bedford into Greene County and then to Switz City. (Courtesy of Dick Fontaine.)

BEDFORD DUST PLANT. This image gives a good look at the dust plant on the old B&B branch west of Bedford. This was where small particles of refuse limestone were ground up into a fine powder. The powder could be used as an agricultural lime to reduce acid in soil or as a base in cosmetics. It was often packaged and shipped in 40-pound bags. (Courtesy of Dick Fontaine.)

Six

THE MONON
IN BLOOMINGTON

BLOOMINGTON MONON DEPOT. This passenger depot was built in 1911 for $25,680 and torn down in the 1970s. It had a tile roof and was a great example of the limestone depots built by the Monon Railroad. The Monon also built these sturdy limestone depots at French Lick, Bedford, Frankfort, and Lafayette. Of these four, only the depots at Bedford, Lafayette, and French Lick are still standing. (Courtesy of the MRHTS.)

MONON PASSENGER TRAIN AT BLOOMINGTON. This image was taken in 1961 and shows F-3 diesel No. 84B moving through downtown Bloomington. This passenger train, the *Thoroughbred*, traveled south from Chicago to Louisville and was designated as train No. 5. Many students at Indiana University relied upon Monon trains as they began and ended semesters and weekend trips. The passenger depot can be partially seen behind the cab of the engine. (Courtesy of Richard Wolff.)

WORKING THE INDIANA STONE RAILROAD. In this undated photograph, Monon steam locomotive No. 524, a 2-8-2, J-1 locomotive, has several loads of block limestone loaded on flatcars. Limestone was big tonnage for the Monon but did not pay as well as other commodities. Monon caboose C-276 is part of this quarry train. (Courtesy of the MRHTS, J. F. Bennett Collection.)

STEAM WORKING LIMESTONE. Much of the Monon trackage in Monroe County had challenging grades in and around limestone quarries such as this one. Hauling stone out of these quarries worked well financially for the Monon in the 1920s but nearly disappeared in the mid-1940s. This image also shows Monon steam locomotive No. 524 loaded with limestone. (Courtesy of the MRHTS, J. F. Bennett Collection.)

ENGINE CONSIST AT MCDOEL TURNTABLE. This photograph shows a portion of the McDoel Yard in Bloomington. To the far left is a portion of the yard turntable. In the center is the yard office. The turntable has long been removed. Engine No. 516, a C-420, is shown heading an engine consist in the yard. (Courtesy of the MRHTS, Ron Marquardt Collection.)

FREIGHT HOUSE. This image shows the most recent Monon Railroad freight house that was located between Fourth and Fifth Streets in Bloomington. It was demolished in May 1966. A Sanborn map of Bloomington shows a freight house as early as December 1887 at that site. It had a ticket office and waiting rooms. (Courtesy of the MRHTS.)

DIESEL NO. 51 AT MCDOEL YARD. This image shows several locomotives in the background and Monon engine No. 51, to the right, an RS-2 diesel. It was photographed near the sand tower in the McDoel Yard in Bloomington. All the Monon's RS-2 diesels were purchased in 1947 from Alco, and the Monon fleet was initially numbered 21–29. (Courtesy of Dick Fontaine.)

CONSIST OF MONON DIESELS. This consist of Monon C-420 locomotives was actually clearing its smokestacks at the McDoel Yard in Bloomington so that the photographer would have smoke for the picture. The front engine, No. 509, was purchased in August 1967, six years after the C-420 was first introduced by the Alco. The C-420 was one of Alco's more successful designs, built from 1963 to 1968. (Courtesy of Dick Fontaine.)

MONON HOPPER AT MCDOEL YARD. This image shows Monon covered hopper No. 52031 while at the McDoel Yard in Bloomington. The image was taken in April 1976, five years after the Monon was merged into the Louisville and Nashville Railroad. It took several years for the Monon rolling stock to be repainted and renumbered into the new scheme of the Louisville and Nashville Railroad. (Courtesy of Jim Craig.)

WINTER VIEW OF THE TURNTABLE. This image was captured from atop a covered hopper showing an RS-2 diesel on the McDoel Yard turntable. Monon Railroad records list as many as 12 buildings at the yard, including a frame sand house and bin built in 1914. The McDoel Yard was the base for locals working the areas south toward Louisville, north to Lafayette, the nearby stone district, and the French Lick area. (Courtesy of Dick Fontaine.)

McDOEL SAND TOWER. This image shows the turntable in the center and the sand tower to the right. Sand was sometimes needed on the rails to improve traction, and sand towers were used to store the sand until needed. All engines were equipped with sandboxes, and the sand was dropped from the tower into the boxes and routed through pipes and sprayed onto the track as needed. (Courtesy of Jim Craig.)

CABOOSES ON PARADE. Four Monon cabooses are on the caboose track at the McDoel Yard. The front caboose, No. 81528, is still accessible to railfans. It is now located at the Indiana Transportation Museum at Noblesville. It was refurbished in the late summer and early fall of 2007 by members of the MRHTS. (Courtesy of Dick Fontaine.)

MCDOEL YARD OFFICE. The McDoel Yard was named for Monon president W. H. McDoel, who served the Monon from 1899 to 1909. This trackside photograph shows the Monon yard office several years ago. The yard capacity was listed at 731 cars and broken down as follows: 13 yard tracks holding 512 cars; 3 repair tracks holding 80 cars; and 6 other tracks holding 139 cars. (Courtesy of Tim Swan.)

MONON RAIL TRAIL. This same yard office was in poor condition in 2004 as the McDoel Yard was being demolished. This image was taken during the 2004 MRHTS's annual tour, when the group toured much of the dismantled train yard and other structures around Bloomington. Today the former train yard is a key part of the construction of the Bloomington Rail Trail.

MCDOEL SWITCH ENGINE. Diesel No. 14 was seen often in the Monon Railroad's McDoel Yard. This NW-2 diesel was purchased by the Monon in January 1947. The McDoel Yard switch engine had several assignments per day, which included handling certain trains, completing yard work, handling the north and south stone trains, and making up trains. Unit 14 was sold in 1970 to the Elgin, Joliet, and Eastern Railway. (Courtesy of the MRHTS.)

BLOOMINGTON CELEBRATES THE
CENTENNIAL. This image was taken
in July 1947, as the Monon Railroad
was celebrating its 100th anniversary.
This celebration lasted a good part of
a week in many of the towns and cities
from Michigan City to New Albany.
The center of attention in this image
is the Civil War steam locomotive the
General, which is at the Monon depot.
(Courtesy of the Monroe County
Historical Society Museum.)

EMPIRE STONE COMPANY. This image was taken at the Empire Stone Company quarry and
shows two Monon gondolas being loaded. In the center is a huge crane used to lift the blocks
from the quarry and also used to load blocks onto the gondolas. A yard truck can be seen behind
the Monon gondolas. (Courtesy of the Monroe County Historical Society Museum.)

WRECKER AT STINESVILLE. This image shows Monon wrecker No. 3 setting an octagonal limestone column on Monon flatcar No. 14191 at the Hoadley and Sons quarry at Stinesville, north of Bloomington. Stinesville is considered the birthplace of the limestone industry and has a commemorative marker that refers to it as the "home of the quarry lads." It is believed that Richard Gilbert quarried Oolitic stone near Stinesville in 1827. (Courtesy of the MRHTS.)

RECORDS HATCHERY. This image, taken on December 12, 1967, shows a Monon diesel approaching the Records Hatchery, on the left. Records Feed received grain shipments on an average of 22 railcars per year in the late 1950s. The hatchery was located at North Morton Avenue and Seventh Street. (Courtesy of Dave Ritenour.)

SHOWERS BROTHERS FURNITURE PLANT. This image shows Showers Brothers Furniture Plant No. 1 on West Eighth Street. It was built after an 1884 fire destroyed the original plant. One of the more noticeable features about the plant is the sawtooth roofline. The plant was served by the Monon Railroad in its early years and by the Illinois Central Railroad after 1906. (Courtesy of the Monroe County Historical Society Museum.)

SHOWERS FACTORY WORKERS. This image shows several men working in the Showers Brothers Furniture Plant No. 1 machine shop. Heavy denim coveralls, like the ones worn by these workers, were a common mode of dress with factory workers in this era. In 1912, Showers Brothers was considered the largest furniture manufacturer in the world. (Courtesy of the Monroe County Historical Society Museum.)

HISTORIC SHOWERS PLAZA. This image shows a portion of the Showers Brothers Furniture Plant No. 1 at 350 Morton Street as it looks today. It was built in 1910 and designed by Chicago architect C. H. Ballew. The plant was constructed of concrete and brick walls with hard maple floors. It was considered nearly fireproof because it had water sprinkler heads about 10 feet apart. Other buildings of this factory complex were destroyed in a fire in 1966. Showers at one time had four building sites and over a dozen accessory buildings on seven acres. The building had multiple uses, which included housing the planing mill, the garage, the furniture showroom, and the company offices. In recent years, Indiana University and the City of Bloomington developed a plan to revitalize the buildings. The plant was renovated by CFC, Inc., and is now known as Historic Showers Plaza. It is the home of the Bloomington City Hall and used by the Indiana University Research Park.

RADIO CORPORATION OF AMERICA. This image is familiar to anyone who has worked as an hourly employee at a factory. After the horn blows, workers head for the time clocks to "clock out" as they leave work. This late-1940s scene was at the Radio Corporation of America (RCA) plant at 1300 South Rogers Street. This building had been built in 1919 for the Showers Brothers Furniture Company. The plant was sold to RCA in 1939, when Bloomington became home to the RCA Home Instruments Division. In June 1940, the first radio was produced at the Bloomington factory. From 1940 to 1968, employment grew from 200 to more than 6,000. In 1986, RCA was purchased by General Electric (GE). The next year, GE sold its RCA and GE consumer electronics businesses to Thomson Consumer Electronics, a France-based company. By April 1998, Thomson had closed. Many of the plant buildings have been demolished. However, Cook Pharmaceutical has renovated a large warehouse into a manufacturing facility. (Courtesy of the Monroe County Historical Society Museum.)

RCA LOADING DOCK. This 1940s image shows the loading dock of the RCA plant and one of its delivery trucks off South Rogers Street. The driver is in the truck and on the truck's side panel and door can be seen the famed RCA symbol, Nipper the dog. In 1898, Nipper, who died in 1896, served as the model for a painting entitled *His Master's Voice*, by Francis Barraud. Francis was the brother of the dog's original owner, Mark Barraud, who died in 1897. Nipper's likeness later became identified with RCA Records. The slogan "His Master's Voice" and a painting of the dog were sold to the Gramophone Company for £100. Nipper's image, as seen on phonographs, radios, and other small appliances, is one that many Americans still cherish as a symbol of America's strength in manufacturing. (Courtesy of the Monroe County Historical Society Museum.)

RCA RECORD PLAYER. This image shows two ladies in an advertisement promoting a long-play RCA Victor phonograph. The image was taken in the 1940s and also shows the record-changing ability of the small appliance. Phonographs were just one of many electronic products produced at the plant in Bloomington. In 1949, the Bloomington plant turned out its first television set. RCA also chose the Bloomington plant to produce its highly innovative and complex color television sets when first introduced in March 1954. During these years, the plant expanded from 225,000 square feet to over 1.4 million square feet, with 22 buildings. Limited records show that in the late 1950s, the Monon Railroad delivered over 1,400 train cars to the RCA plant annually. During those same years, RCA shipped an average of over 140 train cars of product with the Monon Railroad. (Courtesy of the Monroe County Historical Society Museum.)

JOHNSON CREAMERY. Johnson Creamery was first located at 224 Morton Street, and the Monon Railroad shipped coal and boxes to the creamery. The creamery provided a complete line of dairy products. These products were delivered in trucks like the one at the loading dock. The restored building located at 400 West Seventh Street is on the National Register of Historic Places. (Courtesy of the Monroe County Historical Society Museum.)

JOHN R. FIGG WAREHOUSE. In 1928, John R. Figg opened a small building at 215 West Eighth Street for his produce business. By 1932, business had prospered and the business moved to 222 West Seventh Street. In the late 1950s, Figg received food products by rail and was served by the Monon Railroad. This 1940s image shows the Figg Wholesale Grocery warehouse. (Courtesy of the Monroe County Historical Society Museum.)

WESTINGHOUSE PLANT. This 1970s image shows the two-story, flat-roofed Westinghouse plant that was completed in 1957 at 341 North Curry Pike. The Westinghouse Apparatus Division had relocated to Bloomington from East Pittsburgh, Pennsylvania. The plant manufactured electrical equipment such as capacitors, lightning arrestors, switches, and breakers. The Monon shipped products for Westinghouse and delivered parts to it beginning in the late 1950s. (Courtesy of the Monroe County Historical Society Museum.)

WEGMILLER-DAVIS LUMBER OFFICE. Wegmiller-Davis Lumber Company, a Monon customer, was founded in the fall of 1931 by Harold Wegmiller and Fullwater Lumber Company employee Sylvester Davis. This partnership dissolved five years later, and Harold Wegmiller was managing alone. His first new hire was Harold Bender, who remained there for 27 years. This image, taken in 1959, is looking north and shows the office on West Eleventh Street. (Courtesy of John Bender.)

WEGMILLER-BENDER LUMBER COMPANY. In 1963, Harold Wegmiller sold the company to Harold Bender. In the late 1960s and early 1970s, it was named Wegmiller-Bender Lumber Company and enlarged its buildings and property south of Eleventh Street. It soon increased its inventory to include hardware, kitchen products, and other consumer products. During the 1970s, the name changed to Bender Lumber Company, which now has locations in several other southern Indiana cities.

BLACK LUMBER COMPANY. The original Black Lumber Company was located at 337 South Madison Street and was begun by Joseph Black. This image shows the company offices to the right and the loading dock. In the late 1950s, the Monon shipped an average of 70 railcars to Black Lumber annually. The lumber company is now located at 1710 South Henderson Street. (Courtesy of C. E. Taylor, Black Lumber Company.)

BIBLIOGRAPHY

American Legion Post 203. *History of Pekin, Indiana.* Self-published, 1959.

"City of Bloomington Interim Report." Bloomington, IN: City of Bloomington, 2004.

Coats, Norman M. *Growing Up on Daisy Hill.* Kirkwood, MO: Self-published, 2001.

Dolzall, Gary W., and Stephen F. Dolzall. *Monon, The Hoosier Line.* Bloomington: Indiana University Press, 1987.

Guthrie, J. M. *History of Lawrence County.* Greenfield, IN: Mitchell-Fleming Publishing Company, 1958.

Hilton, George. *Monon Route.* La Jolla, CA: Howell-North Books, 1978.

Lawrence County Historical Society. *History of Lawrence County.* Paducah, KY: Turner Publishing Company, 1990.

Lewnard, Ed. *Monon in Color.* Scotch Plains, NJ: Morning Sun Books, 2002.

McDonald, Bill. *A Short History of Indiana Limestone.* Bedford, IN: Self-published, 1995.

Mitchell Centennial, Inc. *100 Years of Progress: 1853–1953, Mitchell's Journal of Memories.* Mitchell Centennial, Inc., 1953.

Paoli Chamber of Commerce. *History of Orange County, 1826–1991.* Paducah, KY: Turner Publishing Company, 1992.

Simons, Richard S., and Francis H. Parker. *Railroads of Indiana.* Bloomington: Indiana University Press, 1997.

Washington County Historical Society. *History of Washington County.* Evansville, IN: Unigraphic Inc., 1976.

Wilson, W. E. *A History of the Borden Institute.* Vol. 4. Terre Haute, IN: Teachers College Press, 1931.

Visit us at
arcadiapublishing.com